TAMALES

TAMALES

Daniel Hoyer
Photographs by Marty Snortum

Salt Lake City | Charleston | Santa Fe | Santa Barbara

First Edition
08 09 10 11 12   5 4 3 2 1

Published by
Gibbs Smith
P.O. Box 667
Layton, Utah 84041

1-800.835.4993 orders
www.gibbs-smith.com

Designed and produced by Natalie Peirce
Printed and bound in China

Library of Congress Cataloging-in-Publication Data

Hoyer, Daniel.
Tamales / Daniel Hoyer ; photographs by Marty
Snortum. — 1st ed.
p. cm.
ISBN-13: 978-1-4236-0319-1
ISBN-10: 1-4236-0319-2
1. Cookery, Mexican. 2. Stuffed foods (Cookery) 3.
Cookery (Corn) I. Title.
TX836.H69 2008
641.5972—dc22
2008007988

This book is dedicated to my family.
Your patience and support help
to make it all possible.

I would like to thank the countless tamale cooks that have fed and informed me on my journey to learn this special skill. I also want to acknowledge the cookbook authors that have blazed the trail ahead of me, especially Diana Kennedy, Rick Bayless, and Mark Miller. Special thanks to Noe Cano for many great hours in the kitchen, the use of your steamer and your friendship. Ian, your memory helps to keep me moving forward; I feel your presence looking over my shoulder whenever I am in the kitchen.

Contents

Introduction

Tamales have been shown to originate in Mesoamerica as early as 5000 to 8000 BC, and they invoke different memories for many people. Those of Latino heritage may have grown up with tamales and consider them a regular part of their culinary heritage. Others may have first encountered them as a street food in the border towns and in areas where there are large populations of Mexican Americans. These days, tamales remain an important part of the traditions of Mexico, Central and South America, and the southwestern United States. Tamales have also been popular in Mississippi, New York, and Chicago, where they were often known as "red hots," since the turn of the twentieth century. This Delta tradition started when migrant Mexican workers were brought in to work alongside the African Americans in the cotton fields of the South. Tamales have endured for a millennium and seem to have become more popular recently as part of a renaissance in Latin American and Mexican cooking.

The word *tamal*, the proper singular form, derives from the Nahuatl word *tamalii*. Aztec and Maya civilizations as well as the Olmeca and Tolteneca before them used tamales as a portable food, often to support their armies but also for hunters and travelers. Historical records indicate that the conquistadores were served tamales at some of their earliest encounters with Mesoamerican civilizations. There have also been reports of tamale use in the Inca Empire long before the Spanish visited the New World.

Tamales prepared with animal fats like pork lard are often too rich and calorie-laden for everyday eating in today's societies, so they have become more of a celebratory food. You will see tamales served for holidays like Christmas, New Year's, Day of the Dead, birthdays, weddings, and baptisms. In ancient history, there were countless fillings used in tamales; however, in the recent past, the varieties narrowed down considerably and, in some places, meat with green or red chile was the typical tamale seen. Today, we are seeing a growth of interest in tamales that has resulted in the reemergence of some of the more traditional varieties and the invention of new types.

In this book, I have endeavored to give an overview of the ingredients, methods of preparation, and flavor possibilities of tamales. I have included three different types of masa with variations on each of those, a variety of fillings and enough sauce and salsa recipes to keep you making tamales for a long time. I also hope that the information contained herein will inspire you to try your own hand at creating recipes and will encourage further exploration of the subject through practice, travel to areas known for tamale making, additional reading and research, and discussion with other cooks. Tamale making often will become a social occasion. Since the steps can be long and somewhat tedious, many people like to get together as a community group to prepare the tamales needed for large celebrations. This ongoing tradition in Latin America is called a *Tamalada* and is also practiced in Latino communities in the United States. The stories and gossip alone are enough to attract a large crew of helpers. Many of my students like to organize tamale parties with a good portion of the components prepared in advance (or each guest is responsible for bringing one part of the recipe), and then the tamales are assembled and cooked at the party by the guests. This can be a lot of fun, and it is a practical solution to spending the day alone in the kitchen. Whether you are cooking for a few friends or family, for a special occasion or holiday, in a restaurant or for a tamale party you're hosting, I wish you a hearty *¡Buen Provecho!*

Necessary Items and Techniques for Making Tamales

Equipment

Much of the equipment required for making tamales may be improvised; however, a few basic items will make the job much easier.

Mixer: Although not absolutely essential, I would probably not make very many tamales without one to assist me. Beating the masa by hand is not only tiring, it does not result in as nice a texture as the machine-whipped method. If you opt for whipping the masa by hand, lay in a good supply of large and sturdy wooden spoons. I prefer a heavy-duty stand mixer with a strong motor. Most of the brands come in 5- and 6-quart sizes. When using a 6-quart, the whole process speeds up by about half because of the more powerful motor. The larger capacity is also nice for making

larger recipes or for doubling up to serve a crowd. While a hand mixer will do the job much faster than by hand, it is considerably slower than the stand type.

Steamer: Tamale steamers of many different materials and in a wide variety of shapes and sizes are readily available at Latin American stores and online. Stacking bamboo steamers for Asian cooking may also be used, and the metal, Thai-style stacking steamer is excellent for preparing large quantities. I have also had success with a pasta cooker that has an insert for draining and removing the pasta. Any large pot with a way to keep the tamales above the water in the bottom will work. You will need a pot that is at least 12 inches in diameter and over 14 inches tall, with a liquid capacity of more that 2 gallons that will accommodate at least 3 dozen, medium-sized tamales. Rather than grapple with a huge pot, I use several normal-sized steamers when preparing large quantities.

Mixing bowls: You will need several good-sized bowls to mix and hold the ingredients while preparing tamales.

Strainers: A strainer is useful in preparing many of the sauces needed for tamales. A "China cap" type of strainer is my favorite although the various types of wire mesh strainers also work fine.

Blender and/or food processor: These are very useful to make many of the sauces for the tamales. You could use a *molcajete* for many; however, it can be a bit cumbersome.

Cooking pots and pans: In order to prepare the sauces, fillings, and broths used in these recipes, several of these are very important: a heavy-duty skillet for roasting onions, garlic, tomatoes, and tomatillos; a heavy pot or Dutch oven for frying and for cooking many of the sauces; a roasting pan with a cover (or use foil) to cook some of the fillings and several of the tamales; a large pot (at least 2½-gallon capacity) for making broth/stock.

Measuring spoons and cups: These are necessary for measuring ingredients and portioning the components of the tamales. A kitchen scale is also a handy piece of equipment for some of the measuring.

Mixing/stirring spoons and spatulas: I use several large spoons, both metal and wooden, for stirring, mixing, and portioning. Rubber spatulas are useful for spreading masa, as are large table/soup spoons (not measuring spoons). I find the commercial masa spreaders to be useless because they feel awkward and do not effectively spread the masa the way I like, but you may feel differently.

Tongs: These are very useful for placing tamales in and removing them from the steamer.

Ingredients

Only your own preferences and creativity will limit the ingredients that may be used for tamales. Once you have mastered the basics you should feel free to try new additions and develop your own recipes. The following section will discuss the basic ingredients that are used in most tamales.

Corn: Corn is the universal ingredient of the dough in traditional tamales. Field corn varieties are used; sweet corn does not contain sufficient starch and is not the right

flavor. Although a number of different colors of corn are used in tamale making—red, yellow, blue, black, etc.—the most common is a white variety called *maize blanco*, known as *cacahuazintle* in Mexico.

For the corn to perform properly in tamale and tortilla production, and to make the corn more nutritious to humans, it is treated with an alkali to convert it into a more usable form. Originally, the indigenous peoples of the Americas used the ashes from the cooking fires to accomplish this *nixtamalization*, as the process is known. Today, the mineral lime (Cal), or slaked lime, is the preferred ingredient to treat the corn, although I have seen ashes still used by some traditional cooks in Mexico. Corn that has been nixtamalized, when eaten along with legumes like beans, contains all of the essentials to support human life.

To treat the corn, it is heated in water containing the slaked lime, and then soaked and rubbed to clean it of its outer skin; sometimes the pedicel, or little brown tip, is removed also. The treated corn is then immediately ground to make fresh masa or masa *refrigerada*, or it is dried and later ground to make dry-ground masa, a type of textured corn flour that produces a spongy cake-like masa in tamales. Freshly ground tortilla masa may also be used for tamales. There are also a number of brands of masa harina, commercial dry flour that is mixed with water or broth to make tortillas and tamales, a sort of "instant" masa mix.

Fats: Pre-Columbian tamales contained little or no fat since domesticated animals like the pig were introduced to the New World by the Spanish. Prior to that, the only sources of fat were the animals that were hunted, seeds, and nuts. The addition of animal fats added new dimensions of flavor, richness, texture, and calories. The extra calories were an important bonus when the tamales were carried as a portable food. They would sustain hunters, travelers, and warriors with a minimum amount of weight. Today, due to the richness of traditional tamales, they are usually reserved for special occasions and celebrations.

Pork lard: This is the customary fat used in tamale making. It provides rich flavor and excellent texture, and is readily available in cultures where consumption of pork is popular. Vegetable oils and shortening are also used at times, and butter is another possible substitute. I find that vegetable oils do not lend much flavor, and the texture that results from making tamales with them are not the best. Shortening has the same flavor challenges as oil but does make acceptable textures. I usually combine butter and shortening when I want a substitute for lard, as that yields a texture and flavor that is satisfactory to me. I have run across tamale recipes that use potatoes,

yams, or squash in the masa instead of any fats; however, in my humble opinion, they are not really tamales and are not found in this book. Tamales are not a low-fat fare, and I prefer to save them for the special times that call for a rich food.

Wrappers: Tamales may be wrapped in dried or fresh corn husks, corn leaves, banana leaves, and the leaves of several other tropical plants like avocado. Banana leaves may be used fresh, or they may come frozen when purchased at Latin American or Asian groceries. Dried corn husks must be soaked before using to make them pliable. Banana leaves should be toasted, steamed, or boiled to make them flexible and to prevent splitting when they are handled. I prefer to toast the banana leaves, as I feel it makes for a better flavor in the tamales. I have also seen heat-resistant parchment paper used to wrap tamales, but

I feel that it should be a last resort as the paper does not impart any flavor and doesn't absorb extra fat very well.

Liquids: Along with the corn and fats that make up the masa, liquids are added to create the desired texture and to also add flavor. These liquids include water, meat, chicken or seafood broth, milk, cream, coconut milk, and fruit juices.

Fillings: Fillings for tamales include meat, poultry, seafood, wild game, seeds, nuts, fruit, vegetables, chiles, cheese, and even chocolate. Sometimes leftovers from other meals are employed to fill tamales, and at other times the filling is made specifically for tamale use.

Sauces and Salsas: Sauces and salsas are often added along with a filling to enhance the flavor and to add moisture. These may be chile sauces, moles, gravy-like concoctions like Maya Kol, or tomato sauces (with or without chiles).

Techniques

Masa Preparation

Basic Masa: Masa for tamales starts with *nixtamalized* corn, or corn that has been treated with an alkali like mineral lime, or calcium carbonate. Masa is made from ground freshly treated corn kernels or from masa harina, which is dry flour made from treated corn that has been reconstituted with warm water.

Fats: With the exception of a few pre-Columbian-style recipes, modern-day tamales have fats added to the masa to improve the texture and to add flavor and richness. The choices include pork lard, butter, or vegetable shortening. I have tried recipes using vegetable oil but found that it does not contribute much flavor, and the texture is only acceptable at best.

Pork lard is traditional, with homemade lard or lard produced by Mexican *carnecerías* or Latin American markets providing the most flavor. To make lard at home, render uncured pork fatback in the oven or on the stovetop until it stops popping and hissing, indicating all of the moisture has been cooked out. The color can range from clear to golden brown, depending on how long you cook it. You may also collect lard by skimming it from the pan after you have roasted fatty cuts of pork. The lard produced this way will usually have more color and will carry some of the seasonings used in roasting the pork—perfect for tamales. Store homemade lard in the refrigerator or freezer until you are ready to use it.

Butter and/or vegetable shortening is used to provide different flavors or to substitute for pork in some vegetarian recipes and in sweet tamales. Vegetable shortening gives the masa all of the texture of lard but does not add much flavor, while butter adds flavor and richness but not quite as nice a texture. I often use the two in combination to get both flavor and texture that is acceptable.

Beaten/Whipped Masa: This method of making masa is the one most commonly used in the northern half of Mexico and generally in the United States. The fat is incorporated into the masa by beating it into the corn alternately with liquids such as water, broth, and chile sauces. Hand-beating with a stout spoon is the traditional method, although the use of a hand-held or, ideally, a stand mixer speeds up the process considerably and results in the lightest texture possible. This vigorous beating of the masa with the liquids and fats creates an emulsion that traps air that allows the steam from the moisture to expand during the cooking, resulting in a fluffy tamale masa.

Cooked Masa: In this method, commonly employed in southern Mexico and Central America, the corn masa is cooked along with the liquids and any seasonings, and then the fat is melted and stirred into the masa, resulting in a creamier custard-like texture. The cooking is similar to the technique used in preparing polenta. A heavy pot with a capacity that is two to three times the volume of the masa is useful to help contain the mixture while cooking and stirring.

Vegetarian Masa: Any masa recipe for tamales may be made vegetarian by substituting butter and/or vegetable shortening for the pork lard or by using only vegetable shortening for a vegan version. Substitute vegetable broth or water for meat broth in the recipe.

Wrappers and Ties

Most tamales are wrapped either in dried corn husks or in banana leaves. If you cannot find one, you can always substitute the other.

Dried corn husks need to be soaked before using to make them pliable. Place the husks in a bowl or pan deep enough to submerge the husks and add enough water (hot water speeds the process) to completely cover. Soak for at least 1 hour and up to overnight. When using, make sure to drain and wipe off the excess water.

Banana leaves may be found in Mexican and Latin groceries or Asian markets, usually frozen. To use, thaw first, rinse well, and wipe dry. Cut into pieces appropriate for the recipe that you are using. Often the fibrous rib that runs down the center of a whole banana leaf, perpendicular to the other lines on the leaf, will still be attached. Cut this rib off the leaf and keep it, as it makes for a very strong tie. The leaves need to be lightly toasted or parboiled before filling to make them pliable and to prevent splitting. Toasting imparts more flavor than boiling and does not require a huge pot of water. Toast over a direct flame, on an electric stove burner set to high, or on a hot comal for a few seconds. You will notice the color of the leaf change slightly as heat is applied. The surface of

the banana leaf will develop a shiny quality as it is toasted. Do not over toast, as this will cause the leaf to be brittle. Cover the toasted leaves with a damp towel until you are ready to use them. NOTE: Fresh leaves also need toasting to make them pliable.

To create ties for securing the tamale wrappers, start with soaked corn husks or toasted banana leaves. For corn husks, tear off ¼-inch-wide strips along the length of the corn husk parallel to the ridges that are on the husk. Keep them under a moist towel to maintain flexibility until you are ready for them. If the strips are too short to tie around the tamale, simply tie two together securely.

For banana leaves, tear off ¼-inch-wide strips along the length of the leaf parallel to the lines that run the length of the leaf. Keep them under a moist towel to maintain flexibility until you are ready for them. Again, if the strips are too short to tie around the tamale, simply tie two together securely. The ribs that you cut off the banana leaf will also make excellent ties (see above). NOTE: Kitchen twine or string may also be used to tie your tamales.

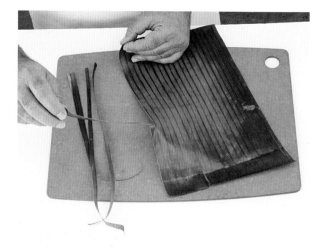

Assembly

Spreading the Masa

For corn husks: Use a presoaked husk that has been wiped dry and place it smooth side up (towards the filling) on a work surface or table. Place the desired amount of prepared masa centered on the widest portion of the husk.

With a spoon or spatula, spread the masa evenly over half to two-thirds of the widest portion of the husk. NOTE: If you want to make double-ended tied tamales, center the masa on the husk.

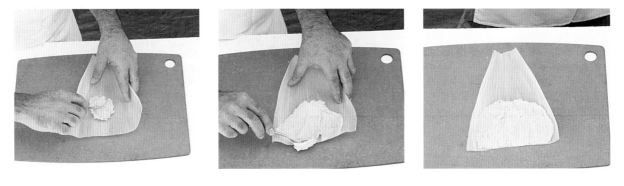

For banana leaves: Use a pre-toasted banana leaf that has been wiped dry and place it shiny side up (towards the filling) on a work surface or table. Place the masa in the center of the leaf and, with a spoon or spatula, spread the masa evenly in a square or rectangle shape centered on the leaf.

Adding Fillings

For tamales made with corn husks or banana leaves: Once you have finished preparing the filling, adding it to your tamales is very simple. Just place a generous amount of the filling in the center of the spread-out masa. Be sure to put equal amounts of filling in each tamale. NOTE: Before adding the filling, you may want to stir in some sauce. See below.

Including Sauces

Sauces in tamales will often be mixed with the filling before it is spread over the masa. If not, you can easily add the sauce on top of the filling after it is placed on the masa.

Wrapping and Tying

There are probably as many different methods for wrapping tamales as there are cooks preparing them. Some have been developed for practical purposes, designed to better encase the type of masa and filling or to utilize materials that are plentiful locally. Others reflect the style of a particular region, town, village, family, or individual. Below are several of the most common methods; please feel free to try other styles that you may encounter or to use your own creativity in developing your own unique style and tradition.

Double-tied-style tamales using corn husks:

1. Fold one side of the corn husk over the filling towards the other side until the edge of the masa on the first side meets the edge of the masa on the other side.

2. Roll the tamale towards where the two sides meet.

3. Grasp one end of the tamale and pinch the end together, giving it a gentle twist.

4. Wrap one of the ties around the end twice and then tie to secure, repeat with the other end, and it is ready to steam.

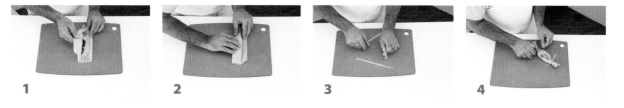

Fold-over-style tamales using corn husks:

1. Fold one side of the corn husk over the filling towards the other side until the edge of the masa on the first side meets the edge of the masa on the other side.

2. Roll the tamale towards where the two sides meet.

3. Hold the tamale so that the seam is centered on the topside facing up. Fold the tail of the wrapper to cover the seam (at least half the length of the tamale). The tamale may now be steamed as is or tied to make it more secure and to dress it up.

4. To tie the fold-over style of corn husk tamale, place a strip of corn husk under the tamale, wrap it around the middle while making sure that you have some of the tail underneath, and tie it securely.

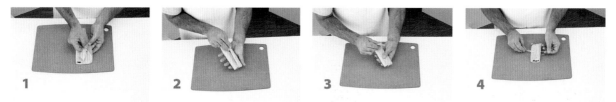

Double-tied-style tamales using banana leaf:

1. Fold one side of the banana leaf over the filling towards the other side until the edge of the masa on the first side meets the edge of the masa on the other side. (For this style you will want to make the masa fully encase the filling.)

2. Roll the tamale towards where the two sides meet.

3. Grasp one end of the tamale and pinch the end together, giving it a gentle twist.

4. Wrap one of the ties around the end twice and then tie to secure, repeat with the other end, and it is ready to steam.

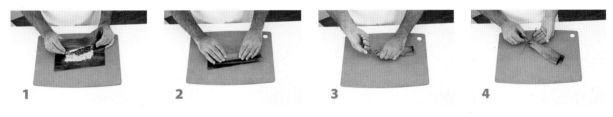

Rectangular- or square-style tamales using banana leaf :

1. Fold the left edge of the leaf to meet the edge on the right. (Often this style of tamale lets the filling be exposed rather than wrapping the masa completely around it. You can make these either way.)

2. Fold the right side back over to the left somewhat snugly.

3. Now fold the bottom flap over the package.

4. Then the top half over that to make a snug package.

5. Place two of the ties in a cross shape and lay the tamale over the top of the ties.

6. Wrap one tie around and tie, repeat with the other, and it is ready to steam.

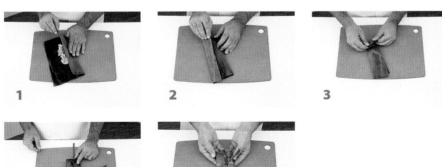

Cooking

With the exception of a few recipes that call for baking in an oven or in a clay pot over a fire, most tamales are cooked by steaming. There are many steamers designed for tamales, and they all work reasonably well. You may also improvise or use some of the Asian-style steamers that are available. The main requirements for a tamale steamer are a pot to hold sufficient boiling water for an hour or more of steaming time (or a convenient way of adding more during the process), a method for holding the tamales above the boiling water that allows the steam to reach the tamales, and a tight-fitting lid to contain the steam.

Place enough water in the bottom of the steamer to last for the entire cooking time if possible. Some cooks insist that adding salt to the water decreases the cooking time and also adds flavor; others say that it is not necessary. I have not noticed any difference either way. Many cooks also place several coins in the pot with the water. These coins will "dance" in the boiling water, making a rattling noise, which tells the cooks that there is still sufficient water in the pot. If the coins become silent, you need more water. When adding water to a pot full of steaming tamales, it is very important that you keep the tamales cooking. It is best to keep a teakettle or other pot of almost-boiling water on hand to add when needed. Never add cold water to the pot while the tamales are steaming! This will cause them to get tough and chewy because of the temperature drop. Always try to minimize the time that the pot is uncovered to help maintain the proper cooking temperature.

When placing the tamales in the steamer, many cooks will position additional corn husks or banana leaves around the outside and over the top of the tamales to help focus the heat of the steam on the tamales, thereby speeding the cooking process. This is not absolutely necessary, but it does help. When arranging the tamales, make sure they are placed in

such a way that the steam can get around and through them to allow for even cooking. They may be arranged standing up or in layers, but do not pack them too tightly.

To test for doneness, quickly remove one and replace the lid on the pot to continue the cooking. Place the tamale on the counter for a few minutes and then carefully unwrap it to check the masa. The masa should be well set and will pull away from the wrapper easily if ready.

Serving

The masa in tamales that have been thoroughly cooked will still be a little soft when first removed from the

steamer. They require a brief "rest" before serving to allow the masa to firm up. You can rest them in the steamer, with the heat turned off and the lid and extra leaves removed, or out of the steamer, covered with a cloth—5 to 10 minutes is usually sufficient.

Typically, the tamales are left in their wrappers, and each individual removes them when serving; extra sauce, if any, is passed around to add more if desired. Sometimes they are unwrapped and a sauce is poured over the top to keep them warm and moist. Either way is fine; just remember that once tamales are unwrapped, they begin to cool quickly.

Storing and Reheating

Tamales will keep for several days in the refrigerator and for months in the freezer. Wrap them tightly in plastic wrap or place in a freezer storage bag to keep them from drying out, or do both. To reheat the tamales, simply steam them again. It should take about 10 to 12 minutes for refrigerated tamales and 25 to 30 minutes for frozen tamales. NOTE: Frozen tamales will have a better texture if they go straight from the freezer to the steamer rather than being thawed first.

Roasting and Toasting

Fire is an indispensable element in Mexican cookery. It is used with a comal or skillet to unlock the flavors of dried chiles, herbs, and other spices, and with tomatoes, tomatillos, garlic, and onions to enrich the taste through caramelizing and charring. Fresh chiles, tomatillos, and tomatoes are also frequently roasted over an open flame, imparting an even more intense smokiness. The extra flavor and complexity achieved by roasting and toast-

ing can be useful to many styles of cooking, not only Mexican. This application of intense heat also reduces the overall cooking times for many sauce recipes, as a long simmering time is often unnecessary for full flavor development. Roasting and toasting is an extremely important technique that can improve the flavors of all of your cooking.

Dry Spices, Chiles and Herbs: Preheat a comal, heavy skillet, or Dutch oven over medium-high heat until you can feel the heat radiate from the surface (the surface should be 350 to 375 degrees). Roast the coarser items like whole chiles and seeds first, followed by herbs and leaves. Finish with ground spices and lastly with ground chiles. Finely ground spices have more surface area exposed to the heat so they are more likely to burn. You will want to finish quickly as the chile smoke is irritating and may cause you to cough and sneeze, so make sure to ventilate well. Stir or toss frequently to allow even toasting; you want to lightly char, not scorch the ingredients. When some smoke appears and color begins to develop, remove the pan to a cool surface. Make sure to wipe out the pan before adding a new ingredient. You do not want to burn the remaining particles from the previous toasting as they will taint the flavors of the new ingredient being toasted. Only toast what you can use in your day's cooking. Toasting releases the flavors, so there will not be much left by the next day.

Delicate "sweet" spices like canela (cinnamon) and cloves have such a volatile flavor that toasting can cause a loss of flavor. I toast allspice when used in savory dishes but not when used in a sweet dish.

Whole seeds may be ground in a mortar and pestle, spice grinder, or *molcajete,* immediately after toasting. Herbs are usually added whole but sometimes are also ground. Whole dry chiles are typically stemmed and seeded after they are toasted, and then soaked in very

hot (180- to 200-degree) water for 15 to 20 minutes to rehydrate.

Fresh Chiles: Fresh chiles are fire-roasted to remove the skin, to begin the cooking process, and to give them a smoky and slightly sweeter flavor. The larger varieties like poblano, New Mexican green, and Anaheim are usually roasted and peeled. The smaller types like jalapeño, serrano, and habañero may be used raw or roasted and charred, and then peeled and seeded (or left intact) for

some sauces and salsas. This method also works for sweet bell peppers (chiles dulces).

Place the chile over a direct flame or as near to a direct source of intense heat as possible (open gas burner, charcoal or gas grill, oven broiler, or toaster oven) and char the skin until at least 80 to 90 percent is blistered and blackened. Rotate often to cook evenly. Place in a paper or plastic bag or in a bowl covered with a kitchen towel or plastic wrap to trap the steam. This will loosen

the skin and continue cooking the chile. After 10 to 15 minutes, rub the chile surface with a cloth or paper towel to remove the skin. I do not recommend rinsing in running water to remove the skin. Although that method is very efficient, the water also removes much of the flavor that you have been working so hard to create. After peeling, the chile may be carefully slit open on one side to remove the seeds before stuffing for chile rellenos, or the stem and seeds may be removed prior to chopping to use in salsa or to puree for a sauce or soup.

You may want to wear surgical or rubber gloves when handling the chiles to avoid burning your skin. Always remember to wash your hands well after peeling chiles; if you forget and touch yourself, you may regret it. A vinegar rinse followed by soap and warm water works well for cleaning chile residue from your hands.

Tomatoes and Tomatillos: Both tomatoes and tomatillos may be roasted or charred to improve their flavor for salsa, sauces, and soups. They may be flame-roasted to impart a smoky, slightly bitter and charred quality or they may be more slowly pan-roasted on a comal, well-seasoned skillet, or baking sheet in a 350-degree oven for a sweeter, more concentrated flavor. Pan-roasting may also be used to blacken the fruits if you desire. This method also produces a more pronounced ripe flavor, useful for those almost-flavorless, pink winter tomatoes.

Tomatillos need to be husked before roasting. Some soak them to loosen the skin and remove the sticky substance from beneath the skin. I prefer to husk them dry and then rinse in very warm water for a few seconds to remove the stickiness.

For flame-roasting, proceed as with fresh chiles until the desired degree of blackness is achieved. If you are

using a pan or comal, preheat to about 325 degrees and place the tomatoes and/or tomatillos in the dry pan over medium-low to medium heat. (The pan or comal should be well seasoned, but do not add oil. You are roasting, not frying.) Turn occasionally but not too often. Remove from heat when blackened or browned as desired, and chop or puree as needed.

Onions: In Mexican cooking, many recipes for salsas, sauces, and broths call for roasted onions. Roasting sweetens the onions, removing or reducing the "hot"

taste of raw onions. Slightly charring the onions will also produce flavor that is complementary to roasted chiles, tomatoes, and tomatillos.

On a preheated comal, heavy skillet, or baking sheet in a 350-degree oven, place ½-inch-thick slices or quarters of onions and roast, turning occasionally, until a golden brown color develops (a little black around the edges is fine).

Garlic: Garlic cloves are roasted whole to remove the raw taste and to sweeten the flavor. Roasted garlic is more subtle in flavor so you usually will need to use more than raw. Peeled garlic will roast quicker and develop a darker color. Unpeeled cloves tend to get sweeter when roasted and stay lighter colored. The choice is yours. I use both methods depending on the flavor I want.

Garlic is roasted like onions, and the two may be roasted together. They require the same temperature; however, the timing may differ. Unlike in Italian recipes, roasted garlic in Mexican cooking is roasted at a higher temperature for a shorter time; therefore, it does not get as soft and mushy, and some firmness remains.

MASA

The masa is the defining element of tamales. It provides texture and a medium to contrast with and to carry the flavors of the filling while also protecting it.

Though there are infinite possibilities for filling tamales, there are only a handful of basic recipes for masa, albeit with numerous subtle differences practiced by the millions who prepare them. The type of masa used for tamales is determined by the type of filling employed, regional and local preferences, ingredients available, and personal preferences. Some are dense and compact, and, even though they usually include lard, have an almost chewy texture reminiscent of the pre-Columbian varieties common before the introduction of animal fats into the process. Others are rich yet light and fluffy in texture. Another variation is the strained and precooked version that results in a custard-like texture. Additions to the masa may include herbs and aromatic spices, seasoning pastes, chiles and chile sauces, vegetables, broths, sweeteners, and fruit.

The recipes that follow will give you several basic techniques and approaches for typical tamales that will form the basis for most of the recipes in the book. Instructions for additions, variations, and options will be detailed in the individual tamale recipes. Whether you use these masas for the included recipes, to duplicate traditional tamales that you have encountered in your dining experiences, or to create your own original fillings and styles, they will form the foundation of most of the tamales that you may want to create.

Some of the recipes included here and ones you will encounter elsewhere or create yourself may call for the use of a specific stock, chile, sauce, herb, vegetable, and so forth, to be incorporated into the masa. The recipes included in this book will give you instructions on how to adjust for these additions, and you may use them as guidelines when venturing out on your own. The main thing to consider will be the addition of liquids. Usually, you will need to decrease the liquid in the basic masa recipe to balance the added liquid from stocks, broths, or sauces.

Masa for Tamales

It is understandably easy to confuse the term masa, as it has several meanings in Latin-American Spanish. It is basically a paste or dough that comes from ground grains. In our case, we are dealing with corn that has been nixtamalized, or treated with slaked lime. In tamale making, masa will refer not only to the simple dough resulting from grinding treated corn and from reconstituting masa harina into this dough but also to the dough when it has already been mixed with fat, seasonings, and liquids and is ready to use for tamales.

In this book, I will use the phrase "Masa for Tamales" to refer to the simple dough, whether prepared from freshly ground corn or from reconstituting masa harina. You may buy this ready-to-use masa, usually called *masa refrigerada,* from Latin American grocers, some supermarkets, and tortillerías. Be careful not to buy the type that already has lard or other fats added to it—you want to do that yourself; it is often labeled *masa preparada*. You want the pure stuff for these recipes, and the results will be much more satisfactory. You can also treat and grind the corn yourself. If you are so inclined and fairly ambitious, I recommend you spend some time reading *From My Mexican Kitchen: Techniques and Ingredients* by Diana Kennedy. Her section on tamale dough will be most helpful. For the rest of us, the other options are easier and more practical, and save considerable time.

Whether you have the ready-to-use masa or make your own, all you need to do is measure the correct amount and proceed with the recipe instructions. If you are using masa harina, just follow these steps.

3½ cups masa harina

2¼ cups fairly hot water (140 to 160+ degrees)

1. Mix together well the masa harina and water.

2. Cover and let sit for at least 30 minutes. May be refrigerated and kept for up to 2 days. Makes 3½ cups, enough for 24 to 30 tamales.

NOTE: For the masa harina, I prefer the tamale grind or a mix of tamale and tortilla grind, as I find that using only the tortilla grind is too fine for most recipes.

Basic Whipped or Beaten Masa

This method of making masa produces the types of tamales that are most familiar to *Norteamericanos*. It is used for Tex-Mex, southwestern style, northern and central Mexican style, and many of the commercially available tamales in the United States. The final results after cooking can vary from slightly chewy to firm and compact to light and fluffy, depending on the fresh or dry corn or masa harina that is used to start, the amount and type of fat that is added, and the beating method. Some cooks will also add some leavening, usually baking powder, to lighten the texture; however, I am convinced that it is unnecessary if the correct techniques are applied. If you do wish to add baking powder, add ½ to 1 teaspoon while you are adding the additional liquid during the mixing-whipping process.

Sufficiently beating the masa, along with the fat and liquid, is essential to achieving a proper texture, whether using a stand mixer, hand-held mixer, or whipping it by hand. Try not to over beat, though it is preferable to mix too much rather than not enough, as it takes quite a bit of extra mixing to go too far. One tried-and-true method for testing the masa to see if it is ready is to take about ½ teaspoon and try to float it in a cup of cold water. If it doesn't float, it is usually due to insufficient mixing (unless you didn't use enough fat). Simply whip it for a few more minutes and test again. Often, adding a bit more of the liquid from the recipe or cool water during this second mixing will also help with the floating test, as too-dry masa does not effectively trap enough air. Make sure that you do not add so much liquid that you lose the consistency you are seeking, or you will end up with shapeless tamales.

1¼ cups pork lard, butter, or vegetable shortening

1 teaspoon salt*

3½ cups Masa for Tamales (see page 34)

2 to 2½ cups chicken, pork, or vegetable broth

¼ cup chile sauce from the tamale recipe (optional)

*If using typically salty, commercially prepared broth, eliminate the salt in this recipe.

1. Using a stand or hand-held mixer or doing it by hand, whip the lard until it is fluffy, about 1 minute or so.

2. Add the salt and continue beating while adding the masa in 2-ounce pieces (about 1 inch) and waiting a few seconds between each addition while continuing to mix.

3. When about half of the masa is mixed in well, start alternating the masa with the broth until all of the masa is used along with about 2 cups of broth.

4. Add chile sauce or any other additions and whip until light and fluffy, adding more broth if the mixture seems dry.

5. Test using the cold water method (see above) and whip more with added broth if needed.

6. Proceed to fill and wrap the tamales as directed in each recipe. Makes 5 cups, enough for 24 to 30 tamales.

*If using typically salty, commercially prepared broth, eliminate the salt in this recipe.

Cooked Masa

Another type of masa used in many types of tamales in southern Mexico and Central America is cooked before the tamale is assembled and steamed, resulting in a finer, more custard-like texture. This masa is usually wrapped with banana or other local tropical leaves, but good results may be obtained by using corn husks too. The method that I describe here is my adaptation, using dry masa harina or home-ground corn flour; however, the moist, commercially ground masa will work here also. If you do use the commercially prepared masa, just decrease the liquid by 2¼ cups (the amount of liquid added to the masa harina to make the Masa for Tamales recipe, page 34) and then first combine the fresh masa with the remaining liquid, mixing well before heating. I find that either approach works equally well. If you have ever cooked polenta, you will find the method in this recipe familiar.

When making this type of tamale, it is important to have all of the other components ready to go, as you will want to proceed immediately to avoid the masa firming up too much before assembly, unless you are making one of the recipes where this is called for.

3 pints chicken, pork, or vegetable broth

1 scant teaspoon salt*

Seasonings, herbs, and vegetables as called for (optional)

⅛ to ¼ cup chile sauce from the filling recipe (optional)

3 cups masa harina, fine or tamale grind (if using freshly made Masa for Tamales, or commercially prepared, fresh masa instead of masa harina, use only 2¾ cups; see note in introduction)

1 cup pork lard, butter, or vegetable shortening

1. Combine the broth, salt, seasonings, and optional chile sauce in a large metal saucepan and bring to a boil.

2. Whisk in the masa harina a little at a time until well combined.

3. Reduce the heat and cook, stirring constantly with a wooden spoon, for about 3 minutes.

4. Mix in the fat one-third at a time, along with any optional vegetables, until the fat is well absorbed into the masa. (There may be some fat that remains as a coating to the masa, but do not worry as long as most has been incorporated.)

5. Remove from heat and cover to keep warm and moist until assembling the tamales. Makes 4½ cups, enough for 20 to 26 tamales.

*If using typically salty, commercially prepared broth, eliminate the salt in this recipe.

Sweet Masa

Sweet tamales can run the gamut from something for breakfast, a snack, or a dessert. There are a number of traditional recipes and a whole slew of contemporary creations. This is a category in which it is easy to improvise. Here is a basic version used in most of the recipes for sweet tamales in this book, with the variations given in each individual recipe. It is also a great starting point for your own inventions. I have chosen not to use lard here since I feel that the flavor is a little strong for most sweet tamales; however, many Mexican and Central American tamale makers do use it; the choice is yours. You may use butter, vegetable shortening, or a combination of both. I usually opt for the combination as butter lends flavor and shortening makes for a better texture. I always want both.

1¼ cups butter or vegetable shortening or a combination of the two

¼ to ½ cup sugar, brown sugar, or honey

1 teaspoon salt

3½ cups Masa for Tamales (see page 34)

1 to 1½ cups cool water or other liquid as directed in the recipe for tamales

1. Using a stand or hand-held mixer or doing it by hand, whip the fat until it is fluffy, about 1 minute or so; add the sugar and beat 1 minute more.

2. Add the salt and continue beating while adding the masa in 2-ounce pieces (about 1 inch) and waiting a few seconds between each addition while continuing to mix.

3. When about half of the masa is mixed in well, start alternating the masa with the water until all of the masa is used along with about 1½ cups of water.

4. Test using the cold water method (instructions on page 37) and whip more with additional water if needed.

5. Proceed to fill and wrap the tamales as directed in the recipe. Makes 30 to 40 tamales, serves 6 as a main course.

FILLINGS

Just about any meat, fruit, seafood, vegetable, seed, or nut may be employed to fill tamales.

In this chapter you will find some of my favorites, both traditional and contemporary originals, and they will be needed to create the recipes in the tamale section. These filling recipes will also be useful if you decide to put together your own tamale recipes. The amounts called for will correspond either to the recipe in which they are used or to the quantities that are practical, given the product being purchased (i.e., whole chickens, cuts of meat, etc.). Most of these fillings will freeze easily; extras may be used for other dishes, tacos, enchiladas, soups, etc.; and the quantities often may be multiplied or reduced to fit your needs. Many times tamale fillings are made from leftovers, and perhaps these recipes will inspire you to create your own from things remaining from another meal.

Pollo Asado
Oven-Roasted or Rotisserie Chicken

The taste of a roasted or rotisserie chicken can be one of life's simple pleasures. It does not require a lot of fuss to prepare, it can be used for a whole array of menus, it makes for quality leftovers, and the carcass can be used to make a rich stock. Although well-made chicken cooked in a pot makes for a wonderful tamale filling, and a majority of tamale cooks probably use that method, I find that the roasted method lends a more concentrated and complex flavor—thus, it is my first choice. This recipe may be prepared using an oven, an outdoor covered grill by indirect heat, or a rotisserie setup. I keep the seasonings uncomplicated; however, you should feel free to elaborate as it suits your taste or the recipe for which you plan to use the chicken.

6 cloves peeled garlic, 4 coarsely chopped, 2 whole

2 tablespoons olive or vegetable oil

1 (5- to 7-pound) roasting chicken or 2 (3- to 3½-pound) fryers, giblets removed

4 or 5 sprigs fresh thyme, marjoram, oregano and/or rosemary

Salt and pepper as needed to season

1 or 2 teaspoons powdered chiles (ancho, New Mexican, chipotle, etc.)

Twine to truss the legs

1. Mix the chopped garlic with the oil and set aside.

2. Rinse the chicken with cool water and pat dry. Slide your finger under the skin covering the breast to open a pocket. Rub the entire skin surface, under the breast skin, and inside the body cavity with the oil/garlic mixture, and then place an herb sprig under the skin covering each breast.

3. Season the chicken, inside and out, with the salt, pepper, and chile powder.

4. Tuck the wing tips under themselves to prevent burning and tie the ends of the legs together to help protect the breast meat from drying out.

5. Place in a 375-degree oven or in a covered char-grill or on a rotisserie set to medium heat. Roast for 1 to 1¾ hours, depending on the size of the chicken(s).

6. When the chicken is ready, the skin should be nicely browned and somewhat crispy, the leg and thigh section should move easily, almost pulling free with a little effort, and the internal temperature of the thigh should be about 170 degrees. Remove chicken from the heat and loosely cover to rest for 10 to 15 minutes before carving.

7. Cool completely before stripping the meat for tamales. Discard the skin, remove the meat from the bones, and save the bones for making a stock or broth. Makes enough for 30 to 40 tamales or serves 6 as a main course.

Machaca
Northern-Style Shredded Beef

This beef preparation is the basis of many dishes in northern Mexico. Often the beef is boiled before shredding; however, I prefer roasting it to concentrate the flavors and deepen the color. In addition to making a perfect filling for tamales, machaca may be used for burritos, tacos, enchiladas, and many other Mexican antojitos, or snacks.

To cook the meat

1 (3½- to 4½-pound) chuck roast

Salt and pepper to taste

1 tablespoon Mexican oregano, toasted (optional)

1 to 2 tablespoons New Mexican, chipotle, or ancho chile powder, lightly toasted; or 4 to 5 fresh jalapeños, sliced in half lengthwise (optional)

1 teaspoon cumin seeds, toasted and ground

2 tablespoons oil or lard

1 onion, sliced

6 cloves garlic, peeled

2 carrots, peeled and sliced thick

4 to 6 sprigs fresh thyme (optional)

6 bay leaves, toasted

2 cups water

To finish

2 tablespoons vegetable oil or lard

½ onion, sliced in thin strips

3 to 4 Roma tomatoes, quartered, seeds removed, and sliced in ¼-inch strips

Pan drippings from the roast as needed

Dash of mild vinegar or lime juice

1. To cook the meat, season the roast with salt and pepper, as well as oregano, chile powder, and cumin.

2. In a preheated heavy skillet, add the oil and sear the meat well on all sides. Place the meat in a roasting pan and distribute the vegetables and herbs under and on top of the roast. Add the water to the pan, cover tightly, and place in a preheated 350-degree oven.

3. Roast 2 to 2½ hours, or until very tender (check the meat halfway through the process, turn it over, and redistribute the seasonings and vegetables). Reserve the pan drippings; cool the roast and shred with a fork or by hand.

4. To finish the dish, preheat a heavy skillet, add the oil, and sauté the onion until starting to brown. Add the tomato strips and cook for 1 minute while stirring gently.

5. Add the shredded meat and stir, frying until it is heated through completely. Add pan drippings and the vinegar or lime juice to moisten to desired consistency. Adjust the seasonings with salt and pepper. Makes enough for 30 to 40 tamales or serves 6 to 8 as a main course.

Al Pastor
Pork Cooked with Pineapple and Chiles

The term *al pastor* loosely translated means "cooked shepherd's style;" this may have originally been prepared with mutton or lamb, but these days in Mexico, it refers to pork and is usually used as a filling for tacos. The typical commercial method of cooking this involves layering pieces of meat on a rotisserie spit with fresh pineapple and roasting slowly to combine the flavors. The meat is then thinly sliced off the spit to put in the tacos. Pineapples are a perfect contrast with the rich pork and zesty chiles. I have created a home cook–friendly version that is a stew and may be more like the original method. Although al pastor pork is usually used for tacos in Mexico, I find it an excellent filling for tamales.

3 to 3½ pounds boneless pork loin or stew meat, cut into bite-sized chunks

Salt and pepper to taste

2 cups diced fresh pineapple, reserve juice (canned pineapple may be used, but you won't get the tenderizing effect)

Vegetable oil or lard

½ white onion, diced

10 cloves garlic, coarsely chopped

4 to 6 ancho chiles, stemmed, toasted, seeded, soaked, and then pureed

2 guajillo or chipotle seco chiles, stemmed, toasted, seeded, soaked, and then pureed (optional)

3 to 4 Roma tomatoes, well charred and pureed

2 to 3 cups water and reserved pineapple juice (enough to cover the meat)

2 tablespoons pineapple vinegar, apple cider vinegar, or rice vinegar

1 teaspoon whole or ground cloves

1 stick canela (cinnamon) (optional)

½ ounce achiote paste (optional)

1. Season meat with salt and pepper, mix with pineapple chunks, and marinate for at least 2 hours or overnight. NOTE: If using canned pineapple, you may reduce the marinating time to 30 to 60 minutes.

2. Preheat a heavy skillet or casserole on high, add the oil and then the pork, and sear until well browned on all sides. Add the onion and garlic and cook 1 minute more.

3. With the skillet still on high heat, add the chile and tomato purees and fry for 1 to 2 minutes more.

4. Add enough juice and/or water to just cover the meat. Add the vinegar, remaining spices, and achiote paste. Stir well to combine the seasonings and then cover and simmer for 30 to 45 minutes (or bake in an oven at 350 degrees), stirring occasionally and adding water as needed to prevent burning.

5. When the meat is tender, uncover the pot and cook until all but about 1 cup of the liquid is absorbed.

6. For tacos, serve with chopped onions, cilantro, and lime as a garnish, along with fresh corn tortillas. Makes enough for 24 to 30 tamales or serves 4 to 6 as a main course.

Pierno de Cerdo Adobada

Chile-Spiced Roast Pork Leg

A typical preparation with variations found throughout Mexico, the American Southwest, Latin America, and even the Philippines, this yields a tender, rich, and flavorful meat that is easy to shred. The uses for pork in adobo are endless: in a formal meal's main course and for tamales, taco fillings, tortas, and various antojitos. The finished pork freezes well, so the large quantity here can be divided and saved for later use; however, it you prefer to make less, select the Boston butt option, buy a smaller quantity, and adjust the amounts for the other ingredients accordingly. The copious amount of fat that this recipe produces not only imparts an incredible flavor and helps preserve moistness in the meat during cooking, but it may also be saved as seasoned lard for making tamales. Remove the meat from the pan, cool completely, and carefully skim off the fat that solidifies on the top. This lard may be kept in the refrigerator for weeks and may be frozen for months.

6 medium-sized ancho chiles

3 guajillo or New Mexico red chiles

2 to 3 cascabel chiles, or 1 additional guajillo

1 or 2 chipotle or mora chiles (either dried or en adobo)

1 tablespoon whole allspice berries

1 teaspoon whole coriander seeds

½ teaspoon whole cumin seeds (optional)

1 to 2 tablespoons Mexican oregano

1 sprig fresh epazote, 2 tablespoons dried epazote, or several sprigs of fresh thyme and/or marjoram

¼ cup cider vinegar

1. Toast, seed, and soak the chiles in boiling water for 15 minutes, and then drain.

2. Toast the dry spices.

3. Blend all the remaining ingredients except the pork with the spices and the chiles, adding about ⅓ cup or more of water to make a paste about the same thickness as tomato paste.

4. Carefully pierce the surface of the pork leg (both the fat side and the meaty side) about 2 inches deep or to the bone with a paring knife or the tip of a sharp chef's knife. Reinsert the knife in the same place at a 90-degree angle to the first cut to create a cross-shaped incision. Repeat this at random intervals of about 3 to 4 inches apart; about twenty or so total cross-shaped cuts will suffice.

5. Rub the chile paste over the surface of the pork leg, pressing some into each incision.

2 tablespoons honey or brown sugar

1 medium white onion, peeled and
coarsely chopped

8 to 12 cloves garlic

1½ teaspoons salt

⅓ cup or more water

1 (8- to 12-pound, bone-in) pork arm
roast or Boston butt

6. Seal in a plastic bag or in a non-reactive pan and cover. Refrigerate at least 6 hours or overnight.

7. Place in a covered roaster or in the oven in a covered roasting pan and bake at 350 degrees for 4½ to 6 hours, depending on the size of your pork leg. Baste with the cooking juices every 30 to 45 minutes. It should be fork tender and still juicy with some crispy edges.

8. Allow the meat to rest for 20 to 30 minutes before cutting or shredding the pork. This will allow the juices to reabsorb into the meat, making it more flavorful and juicy.

9. You can make a sauce from the pan drippings if you cool it and then skim off the excess fat, as there will be quite a bit. (Save the fat for tamale lard.) The remaining sauce will be rich from the meat and hot from the chiles. I usually strain this to remove any large pieces of chiles and spices. Makes enough for 40 to 50 tamales or serves 8 to 10 as a main course.

Carne Adovada
New Mexican Spicy Red Chile Pork

This is a quicker method for a traditional New Mexican dish that was originally developed to preserve meat before the widespread availability of refrigeration. Now it is a favorite because of the flavor. The traditional method follows below, and you may also create a marinade for chops or tenderloin that works great on the char-grill for a contemporary southwestern twist. Carne Adovada is a hearty main dish and also works well as a tamale or enchilada filling, or as a sauce for chile rellenos.

1 teaspoon ground canela
  (cinnamon)

2 teaspoons toasted and ground
  cumin seeds

2 teaspoons toasted and ground
  coriander seeds

2 teaspoons dried Mexican oregano,
  toasted

¾ cup Chimayo or other New
  Mexican varieties of ground red
  chile (mild, medium, or hot),
  toasted

1 tablespoon honey

4 cups chicken broth, pork broth, or
  water, divided

¼ cup apple cider or sherry vinegar

1 to 2 teaspoons salt, to taste

⅓ cup vegetable oil or lard

1 (4½-pound) pork loin or butt, cut
  into ¾-inch cubes

2 cups diced onions

2 tablespoons minced garlic

2 teaspoons chile caribe, toasted

1. Place the canela, cumin, coriander, oregano, red chile, honey, 1 cup broth, vinegar, and salt in a blender. Blend until thoroughly combined and mixture forms a loose paste.

2. Preheat the oven to 350 degrees. Heat the oil in a large skillet and brown the pork in batches. Remove and set the pork aside. Add the onions to the skillet and sauté until golden. Add the garlic and sauté for 1 minute. Return the pork to the skillet, add the chile caribe and the spice-and-chile paste. Fry for 1 to 2 minutes more while stirring and then add the remaining broth. Bring to a boil to loosen any brown bits that are clinging to the pan.

3. Place in an ovenproof dish. Stir to combine well, cover, and bake for 1½ to 2½ hours, or until the pork is tender. This dish reheats wonderfully and is actually better the day after it is made. Makes enough for 24 to 30 tamales or serves 8 as a main course.

NOTE: The traditional method for making this dish is to mix the marinade together and pour over the meat which is cut into larger fist-sized pieces; cover and refrigerate overnight. Pour the meat and marinade into an ovenproof casserole and bake covered for 2 to 2½ hours, or until tender. The less traditional method above brings out the flavors of the onions, garlic, and pork because the ingredients are caramelized or browned first. Whichever method you choose, the dish is full of flavor and will be a favorite.

Carnitas

Braised, Fried, and Shredded Pork

Literally meaning "little meats," carnitas is a method of cooking pork used throughout Mexico but most famously in Michoacán. Although carnitas is a fairly simple preparation, I have encountered many recipes from cooks all around the country and in the United States as well, so I have created my own from what I consider the best of them. You will notice one ingredient that is somewhat unusual although not at all rare, namely, cola. This is clearly a twentieth-century innovation. Recipes that are more traditional use milk to achieve the carmelization that cola produces so easily; however, the acidity and sweetness of the soft drink also provides an important contrast to the fatty richness of the meat.

Carnitas may be served as a main dish accompanied by tortillas, salsa, guacamole, beans, and/or rice; however, they are also used as a filling for tamales, tacos, burritos, tortas, empanadas, gorditas, etc.

1 medium white onion, peeled and cut into eighths

6 cloves garlic, whole and peeled

2 cups pork or chicken broth, or water

Several sprigs fresh thyme and sweet marjoram, or 2 teaspoons toasted Mexican oregano

4 bay leaves, toasted

6 to 8 whole allspice or cloves (optional)

2 (2-inch) canela sticks (cinnamon) (optional)

1 to 2 chipotle chiles en adobo, chopped (optional)

1 (5- to 7-pound) Boston butt or pork arm roast, cut into fist-sized chunks

Salt and pepper to taste

4 tablespoons pork lard

2 small oranges or tangerines

1½ cups cola or 1 cup milk

1. In a heavy roasting pan (should be small enough that the meat is loosely touching but not tightly packed), place the onion, garlic, broth, herbs, bay leaves, allspice, canela, and chiles; mix to combine.

2. Season the meat with salt and pepper and brown in the lard in a hot skillet. Place meat in the roaster with the whole oranges. Mix the broth with the cola and add to the pan, spooning some of the liquid over the meat to coat.

3. Bake at 350 degrees, loosely covered, for 2½ to 3½ hours, or until fall-apart tender, checking occasionally to ensure there is still some liquid. (Halfway through the baking, turn over the chunks of meat and baste with the liquid.) Cool the meat enough to allow handling and shred with a fork.

4. Cut baked oranges in half and squeeze juice into the pan.

5. Remove the bay leaves, canela, and herbs, and place the shredded meat in the cooking juices, mixing well.

6. Raise the oven temperature to 400 degrees; then bake uncovered, stirring occasionally, until the liquid is absorbed and the meat is well browned, about 25 minutes. Makes enough for 30 to 40 tamales or serves 6 to 8 as a main course.

Picadillo de Cerdo
Minced Pork with Spanish and Mexican Spices

With its roots in Spanish cooking, picadillo has been intermingled with native New World ingredients and regional influences, and is used extensively throughout Mexico. The term picadillo comes from the Spanish verb *picar,* which means "to chop or cut up small." Most cooks use ground pork, but some also use cooked and shredded pork. Variations abound: more or less chiles, more or less aromatics like canela and allspice, nuts or not. Feel free to play around to suit your tastes. Picadillo is not usually served as a stand-alone main dish; rather, it is used to fill such things as tamales and chile rellenos, and, in the Yucatán, to stuff into cheese for the popular Queso Relleno.

2 pounds ground pork

2 cups water

2 sprigs epazote, or 2 tablespoons toasted Mexican oregano

1 medium white onion, chopped and divided

1 tablespoon lard or vegetable oil

1½ pounds ripe tomatoes, charred, then pureed with half of the white onion, and strained

3 bay leaves, toasted

1 cup pitted green olives, chopped

2 tablespoons capers

⅔ cup raisins

1 sweet red bell pepper or green bell pepper, seeded and diced

1 hot yellow jalapeño or serrano chile, seeded and finely minced

1 teaspoon whole allspice, toasted and ground

½ teaspoon canela (cinnamon), ground

A generous dash of ground cloves

¼ cup slivered or sliced almonds, lightly toasted

Salt and pepper to taste

1. Place the pork in a large skillet or heavy pot along with the water, herbs, and half of the onion. Bring to a boil, then reduce heat to medium-low and simmer until it is cooked, about 20 minutes; drain, reserving ½ cup of liquid, and remove the herbs and onion.

2. Heat the lard or oil and fry the pureed tomato and onion. After 2 minutes, add the rest of the ingredients, including the meat and the reserved cooking liquid.

3. Simmer over low heat until the mixture has thickened. Salt and pepper to taste. Makes about 4 cups, enough for 25 to 35 tamales.

Lechón Horneado
Cuban-Style Roasted Pork

A simpler version of pit-roasted pork than Cochinita Pibil, Lechon Horneado illustrates the influence of Cuba on the cooking of the Yucatán peninsula of Mexico. It makes a tasty main dish, or the meat may be shredded to fill tamales or serve in tacos with an array of salsas and condiments.

1 (4- to 4½-pound) pork leg or shoulder

1¼ cups sour orange juice, or 1 cup fresh orange juice with 2 tablespoons mild vinegar or lime juice added

2 tablespoons Recado de Bistec (see page 58)

4 cloves garlic, peeled and crushed

1½ teaspoons salt

1 to 2 tablespoons bottled habañero hot sauce (optional)

1 large banana leaf or heavy-duty foil

1. Make small slices through the fat all over the surface of the pork.

2. Combine the juice, Recado de Bistec, garlic, salt, and hot sauce; rub over the surface of the meat, working it into the slits; marinate for at least 2 hours or overnight.

3. Wrap in banana leaf or foil, place in a roasting pan, and bake at 375 degrees for 2½ to 3 hours, or until fork tender. Makes enough for 24 to 30 tamales or 18 to 24 tacos.

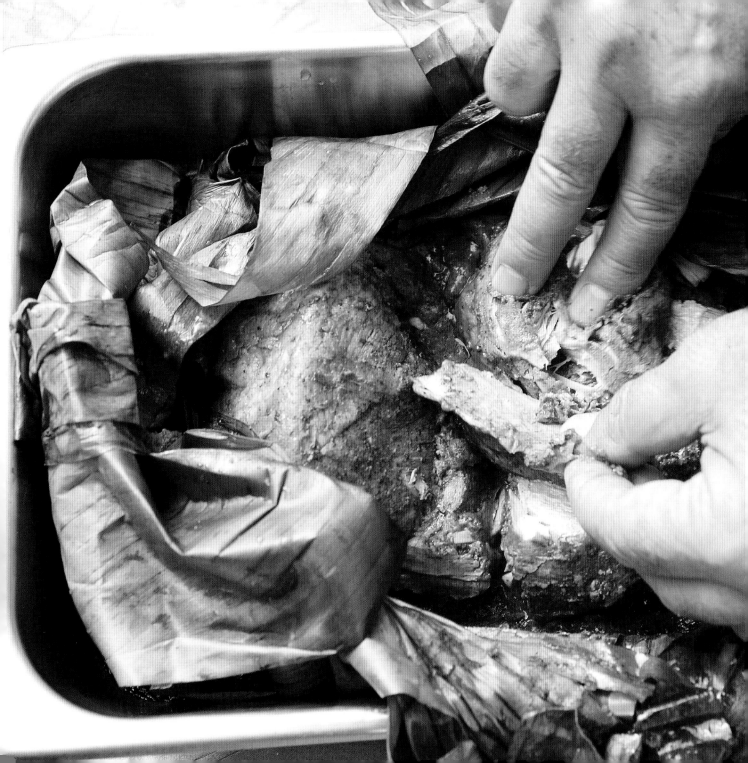

Carne de Cerdo Desmenuzado or Carne Triturada
Basic Boiled and Shredded Pork

Although I tend to favor roasted meats when making tamales, the majority of cooks usually boil the meat since ovens are not an essential piece of cooking equipment in Mexico and Central America, where tamales originated and are still a regular part of the cooking culture. I feel that the roasted version has some flavor and textural advantages to boiling, but the truth is that when combined with a strongly seasoned sauce, as is typical of tamales, the difference is subtle if detectable at all. The searing step is not essential, but I feel that it adds more complexity and richness to the flavor. The pressure cooker option for this recipe is also a great time-saver, and the broth that results from boiling the meat by either method can be used in preparing the masa and some of the sauces. Leaner pork like center-cut loin or sirloin may be used here, but I prefer the flavor of cuts with a bit more fat marbling as it provides better flavor.

2 tablespoons pork fat or oil to sear the meat

1 (4½- to 5-pound) pork Boston butt or arm roast, cut into 3-inch chunks

1 medium white onion, peeled and roughly chopped

6 cloves garlic, lightly smashed and peeled

1 or 2 guajillo, New Mexican, ancho, dried chipotle or other dried red chiles, toasted, stemmed and seeded, or 1 or 2 chipotle chiles en adobo, or 2 tablespoons toasted ground chile

4 bay leaves, toasted

2 to 3 sprigs fresh thyme or 1 tablespoon dried (optional)

1 teaspoon whole black peppercorns

2 to 3 whole cloves (optional)

1 teaspoon whole allspice (optional)

1½ teaspoons salt

Water to cover the meat

1. Heat the fat or oil in a heavy pot or skillet and brown the chunks of meat over high heat.

2. Place everything in a heavy pot, Dutch oven, or pressure cooker; just cover with water. Bring to a boil, cover, and reduce the heat to simmer.

3. Cook for 1½ hours, or until the meat is fall-apart tender (about 25 minutes at 15 pounds in a pressure cooker).

4. Remove the meat from the pot; cool and shred using two forks.

5. Strain the broth and cool. Skim off the excess fat and use in recipes calling for pork broth. Makes enough for 36 to 48 tamales, 50 to 60 tacos, or other favorite Mexican snacks.

Rajas de Chile Poblano
Fire-Roasted Poblano Chile Strips

Chile rajas (rā hās) are little strips of roasted and peeled chiles (usually poblano), that are used as a condiment in many Mexican dishes. New Mexican, Anaheim, or jalapeño chiles may also be used.

3 medium or 2 large poblano chiles, roasted, peeled, stemmed, seeded, and cooled

2 tablespoons lime juice or mild vinegar (pineapple, apple cider, rice)

½ teaspoon salt, or to taste

A few drops of vegetable oil (optional)

1. Cut the chiles into ¼-inch-wide strips.

2. Toss with the lime juice and then season with salt.

3. After 30 minutes, add the oil to help preserve the chiles and to make them shiny. Makes about 1 cup.

NOTE: Rajas are best served within an hour or two of preparation but may be kept refrigerated for several days.

Recado de Bistec
Herbal Seasoning Paste

This peppery paste is not only used in beef recipes as the name implies, but is often called for in pork, chicken, and seafood recipes. The spicy flavor and green color are a nice alternative to the achiote-based recados.

2 teaspoons coriander seeds

1 tablespoon whole allspice berries

1 (1-inch) stick canela (cinnamon)

2 tablespoons whole black pepper

1 teaspoon whole cloves

Pinch of cumin seed

12 cloves garlic, toasted and peeled

1 tablespoon Mexican oregano, lightly toasted, or 2 tablespoons fresh oregano leaves

4 to 5 fresh or 2 tablespoons dried epazote leaves

2 teaspoons salt

Apple cider vinegar, as needed

1. Finely grind all of the ingredients in a molcajete or durable spice grinder.

2. Mix until a smooth stiff paste is formed, adding vinegar as needed.

3. Form into a block or in circular discs, wrap well, and refrigerate to store. Makes about ⅓ cup.

Rajas de Chile Poblano con Hongos
Poblano Chile Strips with Mushrooms

This is a contemporary mix of chiles, onions, and mushrooms that is delicious in tamales or tacos and is a favorite topping for grilled steak at my house. I usually add a bit of butter at the end for the steak topping. Another interesting use would be as a topping on many different tamales to give them a more finished look when serving.

4 medium or 3 large poblano chiles (or equivalent amount of New Mexico Green or Anaheim chiles), roasted, peeled, stemmed, and seeded

3 sweet bell peppers (the color choice is yours), roasted, peeled, stemmed, and seeded

2 to 3 tablespoons olive or vegetable oil

2 cups sliced mushrooms (crimini, shiitake, white button, or wild mushrooms in season)

1 white onion, peeled and cut into long strips

2 teaspoons fresh sweet marjoram leaves, mild oregano, or toasted Mexican oregano

½ cup chicken or beef broth

Salt to taste

1. Cut the chiles and peppers into ¼-inch-wide strips to make rajas.

2. Place the oil in a preheated pan; add the mushrooms when the oil begins to smoke. Sauté on high heat until well-browned and then remove from the pan.

3. Sauté the onion on medium-low heat until golden-brown around the edges (you may need a little more oil for this).

4. Add the rajas, herbs, and mushrooms, and heat through; add the broth.

5. Bring to a boil and continue cooking until most of the liquid is evaporated. Season with salt and serve. Makes about 4 cups, enough for 20 to 24 tamales.

TAMALES

The recipes here will get you started on a lifetime of tamale making.

These are examples of the many traditional and contemporary styles and flavors that you may use for tamales and will serve as a foundation for creating your own combinations too. You will be referred to masa, filling, and sauce recipes from other chapters in this book, but you should also feel free to improvise and choose from other recipes or draw on your own experiences and recipes from others or use your own original ideas to make tamales that suit your taste.

Tamales de Cerdo con Chile Rojo
Red Chile and Pork Tamales

These are the type of tamales that you will encounter in New Mexico and other parts of the Southwest. They are straightforward and fairly easy to prepare, and make a good starting point in a journey of tamale discovery. By selecting red chile that suits your heat preferences, these tamales may be made fiery hot like they are served in the northern communities of Taos, Santa Fe, and Española, or they can be much milder as preferred in other locations. The amount of filling called for will produce meaty, generously filled tamales; some cooks prefer to use less. You could make up to 48 tamales with this amount of meat. Traditionally made with pork, they are also delicious when chicken is used. Another variation is to prepare the Carne Adovada filling recipe (see page 51) and substitute it for the red chile sauce and shredded pork called for here.

24 corn husks plus extra for the steamer

New Mexico Red Chile (see page 118)

3 tablespoons chile caribe (New Mexican red chile flakes), lightly toasted (optional)

Basic Boiled and Shredded Pork (see page 55), or about half or so of Chile Spiced Roast Pork Leg (see page 48)

Basic Whipped or Beaten Masa (see page 37), using the chile sauce option

1. Soak the corn husks to make them pliable (see Wrappers and Ties, page 16).

2. Mix 2 cups sauce and chile caribe with the shredded meat.

3. Spread the masa about ⅜ inch thick on the smooth side of the corn husks to cover the widest two-thirds of the husk to within ½ inch of each side (see Spreading the Masa, page 18).

4. Place 2 to 3 tablespoons of the filling in the center of the masa about ½ inch from the bottom edge (the widest part).

5. Fold one side of the husk over to meet the masa on the other side, roll up, and then fold the tails (see Wrapping and Tying, page 20).

6. Place upright in a preheated steamer pot or arrange on their sides, leaving room for the steam to circulate (use extra husks to cover the tamales in the steamer).

7. Steam for 1 to 1½ hours, or until the masa has firmed somewhat and pulls away from the husk easily.

8. Turn off the heat, remove extra covering husks, and let rest for 15 to 20 minutes before serving. Serve with remaining sauce on the side. Makes 20 to 24 medium-sized tamales.

Tamales de Pollo y Chiltomate
Chicken and Tomato–Chile Sauce Tamales

This is a fundamental recipe for tamales that hails from the central or Gulf Coast regions of Mexico. In these tamales, this recipe uses a bit more masa for each than the Norteño style and sometimes, to keep it white, no sauce at all is added to the masa, a cook's decision. You have several sauce options to choose for this tamale. Usually, all of the sauce is incorporated into the filling, but you may also reserve some or make extra to put on top when serving. I have suggested the double-ended tie system of folding for this variety, but a simple fold over will work fine too.

20 corn husks plus extra for the ties and the steamer

Charred Chile and Tomato Sauce (see page 119), using the jalapeño, serrano, or green chile option, or half of the Chipotle Tomato Sauce (see page 120)

4 cups shredded chicken from Oven-Roasted or Rotisserie Chicken (see page 44), or boiled chicken

Basic Whipped or Beaten Masa (see page 37), adding ¼ cup sauce if desired

1. Soak the corn husks to make them pliable (see Wrappers and Ties, page 16).

2. Mix the sauce with the shredded chicken.

3. Spread the masa about 1 to 1¼ inches thick on the smooth side of the corn husks to cover the center two-thirds of the husk to within 1 inch of each side (see Spreading the Masa, page 18).

4. Place 2 to 3 tablespoons of the filling in the center of the masa.

5. Fold one side of the husk over to meet the masa on the other side, roll up, and then tie each tail with a strip of husk (see Wrapping and Tying, page 20).

6. Arrange on their sides in a preheated steamer pot, leaving room for the steam to circulate (use the extra husks to cover the tamales in the steamer).

7. Steam for 1 to 1½ hours, or until the masa has firmed somewhat and pulls away from the husk easily.

8. Turn off the heat, remove the extra covering husks, and let rest for 15 to 20 minutes before serving. Makes 16 to 20 tamales.

Tamales de Carne de Res Norteños
Tex-Mex Beef Tamales

This is the type of tamale most familiar to many Americans or at least is the type first encountered in their tamale experiences. It remains a favorite but is more common north of the border than in Mexico or Central America, although versions may be found in the northern states of Mexico. They are the sort that you often find on the ubiquitous "combination plate" of "Mexican" restaurants in the United States. This style of tamale probably resulted when past immigrants and their offspring attempted to re-create the tamales from home and were faced with a dearth of the ingredients that they were familiar with and had to adapt to the flavors available in their new homes. Despite their heritage, these tamales remain popular and make up an important part of the Tex-Mex and southwestern culinary landscape.

Although the recipe calls for beef in the tamales, any of the pork or chicken filling recipes will also make for tasty tamales. To fill these tamales, you only need a little less than half of the sauce recipe, although many people like to top them with more sauce after they are cooked.

24 corn husks plus extra for the steamer

Northern-Style Red Sauce (see page 116)

Northern-Style Shredded Beef (see page 45)

Basic Whipped or Beaten Masa (see page 37), using the chile sauce option

1. Soak the corn husks to make them pliable (see Wrappers and Ties, page 16).

2. Mix 3 cups sauce with the shredded meat.

3. Spread the masa about ⅜ inch thick on the smooth side of the corn husks to cover the widest two-thirds of the husk to within ½ inch of each side (see Spreading the Masa, page 18).

4. Place 2 to 3 tablespoons of the filling in the center of the masa about ½ inch from the bottom edge (the widest part).

5. Fold one side of the husk over to meet the masa on the other side, roll up, and then fold the tail (see Wrapping and Tying, page 20).

6. Place upright in a preheated steamer pot or arrange on their sides, leaving room for the steam to circulate (use the extra husks to cover the tamales in the steamer).

7. Steam for 1 to 1½ hours, or until the masa has firmed somewhat and pulls away from the husk easily.

8. Turn off the heat, remove extra covering husks, and let rest for 15 to 20 minutes before serving. Serve with the remaining sauce on the side. Makes 20 to 24 medium-sized tamales.

Tamal de Fríjol Tierno
Black Bean Tamales

These tamales from the indigenous Maya villages in the highlands of Chiapas have no filling. They have black beans mixed in with the masa and are scented with the anise-like flavored leaves of yerba santa, hoja santa or momón as it is called there. I once tried making them with ground aniseed added to the masa, since yerba santa is hard to come by where I live, and I was very satisfied with the results. Serve these tamales with a little Charred Chile and Tomato Sauce (see page 119), or other salsa, or simply use as a side to many meat dishes.

3 cups cooked black beans

30 yerba santa (momón or hoja santa) leaves, or 2 teaspoons lightly toasted and ground aniseed

Basic Whipped or Beaten Masa (see page 37)

30 dried corn husks, soaked until pliable and wiped dry

1. Stir the beans and aniseed (if using) into the masa.

2. Lay out the soaked corn husks, place a yerba santa leaf inside (if using), and spread about 3 heaping tablespoons of the masa over each leaf.

3. Roll up each corn husk and fold the end, or use strips of husk to tie and secure.

4. Steam for about 1¼ hours; let rest for 15 to 20 minutes before serving to firm up the masa. Make about 30 tamales.

Tamales de Pavo Molida con Chile Verde
Turkey and Green Chile Tamales

These comforting and satisfying tamales, although not necessarily traditional, contain many familiar flavors from the Southwest. I use a fairly hot green chile for these as the richness of the masa and the steaming time tone down the heat a bit. Ground turkey is called for here, but ground beef or pork instead may also be used..

24 corn husks plus extra for the steamer

2 tablespoons vegetable oil

½ cup chopped white onion

1 to 2 cloves garlic, peeled and minced

2 pounds ground turkey (not extra lean, as it will be too dry)

¾ teaspoon salt

½ teaspoon ground black pepper

½ teaspoon cumin seeds, toasted and ground

1 to 2 teaspoons toasted chipotle or red chile powder (optional)

New Mexico Green Chile Sauce (see page 122)*

Basic Whipped or Beaten Masa (see page 37), adding ¼ cup sauce if desired

12 ounces grated cheese, such as Monterey Jack, cheddar, queso quesadilla, etc. (optional)

1. Soak the corn husks to make them pliable (see Wrappers and Ties, page 16).

2. Heat the oil in a skillet and sauté the onion until it begins to brown a little; add the garlic and then the turkey. Season with the salt, pepper, cumin, and chile powder, if using, and then fry until the meat is cooked through. Add 3 cups sauce and mix well; remove from heat.

3. Spread the masa about ⅜ inch thick on the smooth side of the corn husks to cover the widest two-thirds of the husk to within ½ inch of each side (see Spreading the Masa, page 18).

4. Place 2 to 3 tablespoons of the filling in the center of the masa about ½ inch from the bottom edge (the widest part).

5. Fold one side of the husk over to meet the masa on the other side, roll up, and then fold the tails (see Wrapping and Tying, page 20).

6. Place upright in a preheated steamer pot or arrange on their sides, leaving room for the steam to circulate (use the extra husks to cover the tamales in the steamer).

7. Steam for 45 minutes to 1¼ hours, or until the masa has firmed somewhat and pulls away from the husk easily.

8. Turn off the heat, remove the extra covering husks, and let rest for 15 to 20 minutes before serving.

9. Unwrap the tamales and then top each with some of the warmed remaining sauce and some of the cheese. Makes 22 to 24 tamales.

*The cilantro option works well here.

Pollo Verde Tamales
Chicken and Green Sauce Tamales

These simple and traditional tamales are always a big hit with my guests. Sometimes I will add some vegetables like potatoes, carrots, peas, squash, and tomatoes to the filling along with the chicken. Either way is good. There is no sauce needed for this variety, but if you prefer it that way, make twice the amount of the Salsa Verde.

24 corn husks plus extra for the steamer

Green Sauce (see page 114)

2 pounds (about 4 cups) chicken from Oven-Roasted or Rotisserie Chicken (see page 44), or boiled chicken, diced in ½-inch cubes

Basic Whipped or Beaten Masa (see page 37)

1. Soak the corn husks to make them pliable (see Wrappers and Ties, page 16).

2. Mix the sauce with the cubed chicken.

3. Spread the masa about ⅜ inch thick on the smooth side of the corn husks to cover the widest two-thirds of the husk to within ½ inch of each side (see Spreading the Masa, page 18).

4. Place 2 to 3 tablespoons of the filling in the center of the masa about ½ inch from the bottom edge (the widest part).

5. Fold one side of the husk over to meet the masa on the other side, roll up, and then fold the tail (see Wrapping and Tying, page 20).

6. Place upright in a preheated steamer pot or arrange on their sides, leaving room for the steam to circulate (use the extra husks to cover the tamales in the steamer).

7. Steam for 1 to 1½ hours, or until the masa has firmed somewhat and pulls away from the husk easily. Makes 24 to 26 medium-sized tamales.

Tamales de Pollo Tlacotalpeño
Tlacotalpan Chicken Tamales

Tlacotalpan is a colorful, picturesque, and historic town along the Rio Papaloapan in Veracruz, Mexico, and has become one of my favorite stops when I am passing through the area. I learned this "secret" family recipe from Carmen Alegre and her husband, Juan, on one of my first visits there. The Alegre family makes several different types of tamales every week to sell on the streets of Tlacotalpan and alongside the main church on Sunday evenings. The recipe calls for hoja santa, or acuyo as it is known in Veracruz; however, it may be eliminated or toasted aniseeds may be added to the masa as a very tasty substitute. If you like, pork could also be substituted for the chicken here. When Doña Carmen creates these tamales, she uses a local leaf as the wrapper. I usually choose banana leaves but have had good success with corn husks too.

Charred Tomatillo Salsa (see page 123), made with 6 to 8 ancho chiles*

2 pounds (about 4 cups) shredded chicken from Oven-Roasted or Rotisserie Chicken (see page 44), or boiled chicken

24 hoja santa (acuyo) leaves (optional)

24 (10 x 10-inch) banana leaves plus extra for ties and to cover the tamales in the steamer, toasted to make them pliable

Cooked Masa (see page 38), made without adding any chile sauce

1. Combine the salsa and the shredded chicken.

2. Rinse the hoja santa leaves and remove the stem and the woody part of the stem that extends into the leaf.

3. Place 1 leaf hoja santa in the center of each banana leaf with the banana leaf's smooth side facing up. Spread 2 to 2½ heaping tablespoons of the masa in the center of each leaf to make a 3 x 4-inch rectangle (see Spreading the Masa, page 18).

5. Place 3 tablespoons of the chicken and salsa mixture in the center of the masa.

6. Roll or fold the leaves to make packages and secure with banana leaf ties (see Assembly, page 21).

7. Place in a steamer and cover with extra leaves. Cook for 1¼ to 1½ hours, or until the masa pulls easily and cleanly from the wrapper. Makes about 24 tamales.

NOTE: If you are not using the hoja santa, you may enjoy the flavor of 2 teaspoons toasted and ground aniseed added to the masa.

*This recipe is usually mild but if you want a little more bite, add a couple of chipotle chiles to the mix.

Tamales de Calabacitas
Tamales with Squash, Corn, and Chiles

Calabacitas literally means "little squash" and usually is a side dish served throughout Latin America. Used in tamales, it makes a tasty vegetarian filling that could be used as a main course or as a side dish. In keeping with the vegetarian theme, I usually use butter and shortening or shortening alone instead of lard in the masa, although lard also tastes fine here. A nice variation for a different flavor and color is to replace half of the masa harina in the masa recipe with blue corn masa harina. The recipe calls for New Mexico Green Chile Sauce, but if you do not have access to New Mexican chiles, substitute Green Sauce (see page 114) or Charred Tomatillo Salsa (see page 123).

24 corn husks plus extra for the steamer

1½ pounds summer squash, such as zucchini, yellow crookneck, Mexican, etc., cut into ½-inch dice

2 cups fresh-cut sweet corn on the cob (about 2 to 3 ears) or frozen corn

1 white onion, peeled and diced

1 large or 2 medium sweet red bell peppers, roasted, peeled, stemmed, seeded, and diced

1 teaspoon salt

½ teaspoon ground black pepper

2 tablespoons chopped fresh marjoram or mild oregano, or 1 tablespoon toasted dried Mexican oregano

Juice of 1 lime

New Mexico Green Chile Sauce (see page 122)

Basic Whipped or Beaten Masa (see page 37), using the shortening or butter and shortening option

1. Soak the corn husks to make them pliable (see Wrappers and Ties, page 16).

2. Mix the squash, corn, onion, peppers, salt, pepper, herbs, and lime juice. Mix in 2½ cups sauce.

3. Spread the masa about 1 to 1¼-inches thick on the smooth side of the corn husks to cover the center two-thirds of the husk to within 1 inch of each side (see Spreading the Masa, page 18).

4. Place 3 to 3½ tablespoons filling in the center of the masa.

5. Fold one side of the husk over to meet the masa on the other side, roll up, and then tie tails with a strip of husk (see Wrapping and Tying, page 20).

6. Arrange on their sides in a preheated steamer pot, leaving room for the steam to circulate (use the extra husks to cover the tamales in the steamer).

7. Steam for 45 minutes to 1 hour, or until the masa has firmed somewhat and pulls away from the husk easily.

8. Turn off the heat, remove the extra covering husks, and let rest for 15 to 20 minutes before serving.

9. Serve the remaining chile sauce warm over the unwrapped tamales. Makes 22 to 24 tamales.

NOTE: If you want to keep the tamales vegetarian, use vegetable broth in preparing the masa.

Tamales de Elotes con Chile Poblano y Queso

Sweet Corn, Poblano Chile, and Cheese Tamales

Throughout Mexico and the southwestern United States, many different types of tamales are prepared using white field corn (elotes in Spanish, or dent corn as it is often called in English). They are known by a variety of names: tamales de elotes, uchepos, corundas, green corn tamales. In most parts of the United States, where we seem to prefer the sweet varieties of corn, field corn is usually hard to come by, and sweet corn does not have sufficient starch to hold the tamales (which are made without masa) together. I will leave you to seek other sources for that recipe; however, here is one that I make, using sweet corn and roasted poblano chiles, that fills the craving for corn tamales nicely. The cheese adds a creamy richness, but it could be optional.

24 corn husks plus extra for the steamer

Basic Whipped or Beaten Masa (see page 37)

4 cups fresh-cut sweet corn on the cob (about 4 to 6 ears) or frozen corn (the white varieties work best here)

1 pound (about 3 cups) grated cheese, such as Monterey Jack, cheddar, asadero, queso fresco, or queso quesadilla, etc.

1½ recipes Fire-Roasted Poblano Chile Strips (see page 59)

1. Soak the corn husks to make them pliable (see Wrappers and Ties, page 16).

2. Spread the masa about 1 to 1¼ inches thick on the smooth side of the corn husks to cover the center two-thirds of the husk to within 1 inch of each side (see Spreading the Masa, page 18).

3. Place about 3 tablespoons corn in the center of the masa. Top with 2 tablespoons cheese and a few of the chile strips.

4. Fold one side of the husk over to meet the masa on the other side, roll up, and then tie tails with a strip of husk (see Wrapping and Tying, page 20).

5. Arrange upright in a preheated steamer pot, leaving room for the steam to circulate (use the extra husks to cover the tamales in the steamer).

6. Steam for 45 minutes to 1 hour, or until the masa has firmed somewhat and pulls away from the husk easily.

7. Turn off the heat, remove the extra covering husks, and let rest for 15 to 20 minutes before serving. Makes about 20 to 24 tamales.

Tamales de Rajas y Hongos
Mushroom, Roasted Pepper, and Poblano Chile Tamales

This original, contemporary-style tamale that borrows from some traditions makes for a creative and striking side dish to grilled meats and seafood, as part of an elaborate holiday feast like Thanksgiving or Christmas, or as the main attraction in a vegetarian meal. Sometimes I will add some interesting cheese to the filling and other times I will leave it as is. For a spicier version, use one of the tomato sauces in this book instead of the tomato puree, or leave it alone, as the flavors in the original, although mild, are rich and enjoyable. The optional epazote leaves will lend it an exotic, truly Mexican flavor, but this is not essential either.

24 corn husks plus extra for the steamer

Poblano Chile Strips with Mushrooms (see page 61)

1 cup tomato puree, or Charred Chile and Tomato Sauce (see page 119), or Chipotle Tomato Sauce (see page 120)

Basic Whipped or Beaten Masa (see page 37)

24 medium-sized, fresh epazote leaves (optional)

1. Soak the corn husks to make them pliable (see Wrappers and Ties, page 16).

2. Mix the chile strips and mushrooms with the tomato puree.

3. Spread the masa about ⅜ inch thick on the smooth side of the corn husks to cover the widest two-thirds of the husk to within ½ inch of each side (see Spreading the Masa, page 18).

4. If you are using the epazote leaves, place one in the center of the masa on each tamale.

5. Place 2 to 3 tablespoons of the filling in the center of the masa (on top of the epazote if using) about ½ inch from the bottom edge (the widest part).

6. Fold one side of the husk over to meet the masa on the other side, roll up, and then fold the tails (see Wrapping and Tying, page 20).

7. Arrange upright or on their sides in a preheated steamer pot, leaving room for the steam to circulate (use the extra husks to cover the tamales in the steamer).

8. Steam for 1 to 1¼ hours, or until the masa has firmed somewhat and pulls away from the husk easily.

9. Turn off the heat, remove the covering husks, and let rest for 15 to 20 minutes before serving. Makes 20 to 24 tamales.

Tamales de Camarones
Shrimp Tamales with Chipotle Tomato Sauce

Shrimp is used in tamales all around Mexico and along the Pacific and Caribbean coasts of Central America. In the Mexican state of Nayarit, seafood tamales are often cooked over a charcoal or wood fire, although they may also be prepared using a traditional steaming method.

For the masa

4 cups shrimp broth, divided

4 cups masa harina

1 teaspoon salt

1 cup (about 10 ounces) pork lard, or 6 ounces softened butter, combined with 4 ounces vegetable shortening

Additional water as needed

For the filling

Chipotle Tomato Sauce (see page 120), using the cilantro option with 3 tablespoons orange juice added after cooking

3 pounds raw shrimp, peeled and deveined (small to medium-sized)

1½ teaspoons salt

24 to 30 (10 x 10-inch) banana leaves plus a little extra to make ties, or 24 to 30 large corn husks, well soaked plus extra for tying and to cover the tamales if steaming

1. For the masa, heat 3 cups shrimp broth to a boil and mix well with the masa harina and salt; cover and set aside to cool.

2. In the bowl of a stand mixer or in a bowl with a hand mixer, whip the lard mixture until fluffy. Add small pieces of masa and continue beating, making more additions until all of the masa is used and adding small amounts of the remaining broth alternately with the masa. The finished masa should be fairly moist yet thick enough that it remains in the spoon when a spoonful is inverted. Continue whipping on high speed until a small piece of the prepared masa floats in a cup of cold water. Set aside in a cool place.

3. For the filling, combine sauce with the shrimp and salt.

4. Toast the banana leaves to make them pliable (see Techniques, page 16).

5. Place banana leaf (or corn husk) on a flat surface (shiny side up) and spread enough masa in the center to make a 5 x 5-inch square about ⅜ inch thick (see Spreading the Masa, page 18).

6. Place about 2 tablespoons shrimp filling in the center of the masa and fold the leaf to make a package that is well sealed (see Wrapping and Tying, page 20). Tie with strips of the leaf to secure. Repeat until all of the filling is used.

7. Place the tamales on the grate of a charcoal, wood, or gas grill, and cook over low or indirect heat. (You might want to use a piece of foil, shiny side down, under the tamales if you have trouble controlling the heat. Another piece of foil loosely placed over top can help to retain the moisture and speed up the cooking process). Turn the tamales every 10 to 15 minutes to cook evenly. It usually takes about 40 to 60 minutes to cook through. Makes 24 to 30 tamales.

Tamalitos de X'Pelon
Tamales with Black-Eyed Peas

X'pelon, or Espalon, is a type of bean similar to the black-eyed pea that is grown in the Yucatán peninsula of Mexico. These beans are added whole to the masa in this recipe, and the tamale is filled with both chicken and pork that is moistened with a "gravy" called Kol, which is made from masa and the cooking liquid. You may use chicken or pork or both.

1½ cups cooked X'pelon or black-eyed peas

Basic Whipped or Beaten Masa (see page 37), adding 2 teaspoons achiote paste, Recado Colorado, or ground annatto seeds mixed with 2 tablespoons sour orange juice or 1 tablespoon orange juice and 1 tablespoon mild vinegar along with the broth

1 pound shredded Cuban-Style Roasted Pork (see page 56), or Basic Boiled and Shredded Pork (see page 55)

1 pound shredded Oven-Roasted or Rotisserie Chicken (see page 44), or boiled chicken

Maya Gravy (see page 125)

30 banana leaf rectangles plus extra for tying, toasted to make pliable

1. After completing the masa float test, fold the beans into masa.

2. Mix both meats with the Kol.

3. Spread masa on each banana leaf to make a 4 x 4-inch square that is ½ inch thick (see Spreading the Masa, page 18).

4. Divide the meat between the tamales and fold to make a sealed package (see Wrapping and Tying, page 20). Secure by tying strips of banana leaf or string.

5. Steam for 1½ hours; allow to cool for 15 to 20 minutes before serving with your favorite sauce or salsa. Makes about 30 tamales.

Tamalitos Chayas
Little Tamales with Greens

Chaya, or *Cnidoscolus chayamansa,* is a plant native to tropical America with a spinach-like flavor and is used by the indigenous people there to provide a nutritional boost since it is high in vitamins and minerals and provides protein, supplementing meat in an often vegetarian diet. Although the flavor of spinach is similar, greens that are more durable often make a better substitute. This version contains pork, but you can easily make a vegetarian version using the instructions in the recipe.

32 (10 x 8-inch) banana leaves plus extra for ties, or 32 corn husks for tamales, soaked

2 pounds chaya leaves or spinach, Swiss chard, beet greens, or collard greens, stems removed and cut into pieces 2 inches across

1 teaspoon salt

Masa for Tamales (see page 34)

1 cup pork lard, or shortening, or shortening and butter (if making the vegetarian version)

Minced Pork (see page 54)

Charred Chile Tomato Sauce (see page 119)

1. Toast the banana leaves over an open flame or on a comal or griddle until the inside of the leaf turns shiny and the leaf is pliable (see Techniques, page 16).

2. Cook the chaya leaves in 2 quarts boiling water with the salt until tender, taking care that they do not become too soft; drain and reserve 1½ quarts of the cooking water.

3. Mix the masa with the cooled reserved cooking water and strain it with cheesecloth or through a fine sieve. Gently heat this in a heavy saucepan or Dutch oven until it comes to a boil and then add lard. Cook, stirring often, for 15 to 20 minutes, or until cooked through and smooth. It is ready when a small amount pressed on a banana leaf pulls away easily and cleanly.

4. Place some chaya leaves on top of the banana leaf rectangles, add 2 tablespoons cooked masa, and spread out about 3 x 3 inches (see Spreading the Masa, page 18).

5. Place 2 tablespoons of the pork on top, cover with another chaya leaf, and form the tamales by folding the sides of the leaf in towards the center; then do the same with the ends until a small rectangular package is formed (see Assembly, page 21). Use strips of the leaves to secure the bundles.

6. Place tamales lengthwise in a steamer. Make sure to leave a little space around each one to allow the air to circulate. Steam for 1¼ to 1½ hours, or until the tamales come off the banana leaf easily when they are unwrapped.

7. Serve tamales on a platter, ladled with sauce, and sprinkle with ground toasted pumpkin seeds and chopped egg or crumbled cheese. Makes 32 to 36 tamales.

Tamales de la Boda Colados

Wedding Tamales

These tamales are customarily served at engagement parties and weddings—hence the title. Colado refers to the straining of the masa through linen or a colander before cooking it and mixing it with the lard. All of this extra effort results in a smooth custard-like texture in the finished masa inside the tamales. In this tamale, the masa is not flavored with any chile sauce, leaving it white to show off the other ingredients that are stacked on top of the masa rather than enveloped in it. These can be made with chicken, pork, or a combination of the two. Unfortunately, they do not freeze very well.

Masa for Tamales (see page 34), reserving ½ cup for the Kol

3 cups water

1½ teaspoons salt

1 cup pork lard

24 (8 x 12-inch) banana leaves plus extra for ties, toasted to make pliable (see Techniques, page 16)

2 recipes of Maya Gravy (see page 125), prepared adding 1 to 2 teaspoons minced hot chiles to the onion when sautéing

2½ to 3 pounds shredded chicken, or half chicken and half pork from any of the pork or chicken filling recipes

1 large or 2 small red onions, peeled and thinly sliced

3 sweet bell peppers, stemmed, seeded, and sliced in thin rounds or julienne

1½ pounds tomatoes, sliced into 24 slices

8 to 10 epazote leaves or ⅓ cup chopped oregano or cilantro leaves

1. Mix the masa and the water until smooth. Press through a coarse strainer or cheesecloth and discard what remains. (You may omit the straining if using the masa made with masa harina).

2. Place in a heavy saucepan with the salt and cook over medium-low heat, stirring constantly until thickened. Add the lard a little at a time. Make sure each portion of the lard is incorporated before adding more. Lower the heat and continue stirring and cooking until the masa begins to pull away from the pan and is smooth and shiny, about 12 to 15 minutes.

3. Pour into an oiled 12 x 18-inch baking sheet or two 9 x 13-inch pans and smooth to make it uniformly thick; set aside to cool.

4. Lay out the banana leaves. Cut the masa into 24 equal squares.

5. For each tamale, place a square of masa on top of the banana leaf, add 2½ tablespoons Maya Gravy, some chicken, an onion slice, the sliced peppers, and a tomato slice, and sprinkle with the epazote or alternative herb.

6. Close the tamale by folding each side to form a package and secure with a tie or string (see Assembly, page 21).

7. Steam for 1 to 1¼ hours. Turn off the heat and remove the lid. Let rest for 15 to 20 minutes before serving. Makes about 24 tamales.

Tamales de Mole Negro Oaxaqueños
Oaxaca Chicken and Black Mole Tamales

For Dia de los Muertos (Day of the Dead) especially, as well as for Christmas, weddings, birthdays, and other special fiestas, black mole tamales are obligatory in both the cities and the villages in the mountains and countryside of Oaxaca. Earlier traditions called for native turkey in the filling, a practice that continues today; however, chicken is more frequently used these days, especially in the more urban communities. Both choices are delicious with the rich and complex black mole. The mole itself is such a complicated and time-consuming process that many Oaxaqueña cooks will make the traditional mole with boiled or roasted turkey or chicken for one special meal and then use the leftovers for the tamales that will be served on another day. The mole is also used to adorn the altars and graves of the dearly departed. It is said that offering these tempting creations will entice the souls of those who have passed on to return and visit during this holiday that is described as a family reunion for both the living and the dead. Banana leaves are the most common wrappers for these tamales in Oaxaca, although I have often seen corn husks (or Toto-moxtles, as they are called there) used instead. Either casing works equally well. Another choice is the type of masa; I have seen both the whipped and the cooked types employed for black mole tamales. Given the time and effort required to make the mole, I have called for more masa here to allow for the creation of a few extra tamales than most of the other recipes in this book. Also, lard is the fat of choice in Oaxaca, the richer the better, but you may opt for the butter and shortening combination as well.

Black Mole Oaxaca-Style (see page 112)

3½ pounds (about 6 cups) shredded boiled chicken, or Oven-Roasted or Rotisserie Chicken (see page 44)*

1½ recipes Basic Whipped or Beaten Masa (see page 37) or 1½ recipes Cooked Masa (see page 28), made without adding chile sauce

42 toasted banana leaves or soaked corn husks plus some extra for the ties and steamer

1. Mix the mole with the meat.

2. Spread about 3 heaping tablespoons masa in the center of each leaf or husk (see Spreading the Masa, page 18).

3. Place 3 tablespoons filling across the center of the masa for each tamale.

4. Wrap and tie the tamales to make a secure package (see Wrapping and Tying, page 20).

5. Place in a preheated steamer and cook for 1½ hours, or until the masa pulls cleanly from the wrapper.

6. Remove from the heat, uncover the steamer, and allow to rest and firm up for 15 to 20 minutes before serving. Makes 36 to 42 tamales.

*Turkey cooked in the same manner may be substituted.

Vaporcitos
Basic Yucatán-Style Steamed Tamales

Vaporcitos means "little steamed ones," and these tamales are the "everyday" tamales served in the Yucatán peninsula of Mexico. The fillings may vary by using pork, chicken, or a combination of the two. For a Caribbean flavor, replace the broth in the masa with coconut milk. While banana leaves are the usual wrapper, soaked corn husks work equally well. Serve as is, with Salsa de Ajo or with some of your other favorite salsa alongside. In some areas, a hot chile (habañero, xcatic, jalapeño, or serrano) is charred, minced, and added to the masa for extra flavor and heat; a teaspoon or two of the Salsa de Ajo is great for this. Feel free to use this basic recipe to create your own favorites. These tamales may be frozen after they are cooked. Place them in a steamer for 15 to 20 minutes to reheat.

1¼ cups pork lard or a mix of butter and vegetable shortening

Masa for Tamales (see page 34), reserving ¼ cup for Kol

1½ teaspoons salt

1 ¾ cups chicken broth, pork broth, coconut milk, or water

Maya Gravy (see page 125)

24 (10 x 7-inch) banana leaves or corn husks, soaked, plus a few extras to make strips to tie and to cover in the steamer

4 cups Cuban-Style Roasted Pork (see page 56), or other shredded pork recipe, Oven-Roasted or Rotisserie Chicken (see page 44), or other shredded chicken recipe, or a combination of both

1. Whip the lard in a stand mixer or by hand until fluffy. Add the masa incrementally while continuing to whip. When half of the masa is incorporated, add the salt then continue with the masa, alternating with the broth until everything has been added and the masa is smooth and fluffy (a small piece should float in cold water).

2. Mix the Maya Gravy with the meat.

3. Toast the banana leaves to make them pliable (see Techniques, page 16).

4. Spread some masa on each leaf about 4 x 4-inches and ¼ inch thick (see Spreading the Masa, page 18).

5. Top with some of the meat and fold the sides of the tamale together to enclose the filling. Then fold the ends to overlap and tie with strips of the leaves, or twist the ends and tie them securely for a rounded tamale (see Wrapping and Tying, page 20).

6. Steam for 1¼ hours, remove from the heat, and uncover. Let sit for 15 to 20 minutes for the masa to firm up. Makes about 24 tamales.

Tamalitos de Pescado o Mariscos del Caribe
Caribbean Fish or Seafood Tamales

This style of tamale is seen along the Caribbean coast of Quintana Roo, Belize, and Guatemala, and at times along the Gulf Coast in Campeche and Tabasco. They are similar to vaporcitos but use coconut milk in the masa instead of meat broth. Any type of fish or seafood will work in these little tamales, alone or in combinations.

Recado Colorado

½ cup annatto seeds (achiote) or ⅓ cup ground annatto seeds

2 tablespoons apple cider vinegar plus more as needed

8 whole allspice berries, lightly toasted

½ teaspoon coriander seeds, lightly toasted (optional)

2 teaspoons whole black pepper

½ teaspoon cumin seeds, lightly toasted (optional)

4 to 5 whole cloves (optional)

12 to 14 cloves garlic, roasted and peeled

1 tablespoon Mexican oregano, lightly toasted

1½ teaspoons salt

Masa

1¼ cups pork lard or mix of butter and vegetable shortening

Masa for Tamales (see page 34)

1½ teaspoons salt

1. For the Recado Colorado, mix the annatto seeds with the vinegar and soak for several hours (if using preground seeds, proceed to the next step without the soaking). Finely grind all of the ingredients in a molcajete or durable spice grinder and mix until a smooth stiff paste is formed, adding more vinegar as needed. Form mixture into a block or in circular discs, wrap well, and refrigerate to store.

2. For the masa, whip the lard in a stand mixer or by hand until fluffy. Add the masa incrementally while continuing to whip. When half of the masa is incorporated, add the salt; then continue with the masa, alternating with the coconut milk until everything has been added and the masa is smooth and fluffy (a small piece should float in cold water).

3. For the filling, dissolve the achiote, salt, and pepper in the juice; add the cilantro and then toss with the seafood.

4. Toast the banana leaves to make them pliable (see Techniques, page 16). Spread some masa on each leaf about 4 x 4 inches and ¼ inch thick (see Spreading the Masa, page 18).

2 cups coconut milk

1 teaspoon achiote paste or Recado Colorado (optional: dissolve in the coconut milk, if using)

Filling

1½ tablespoons achiote paste or Recado Colorado

1 teaspoon salt

½ teaspoon black pepper

4 tablespoons sour orange juice, or 2 tablespoons lime juice and 2 tablespoons sweet orange juice

⅛ cup chopped cilantro (optional)

2½ to 3 pounds fresh fish, shellfish, or other seafood (uncooked), alone or in combination, in bite-sized pieces

24 (10 x 7-inch) banana leaves plus a few extras to make strips to tie

5. Top masa with some of the seafood and fold the sides of the tamale together to enclose the filling. Then fold the ends to overlap and tie with strips of the leaves, or twist the ends and tie them securely for a rounded tamale (see Wrapping and Tying, page 20).

6. Steam for 1¼ hours, remove from the heat, and uncover. Let sit for 15 to 20 minutes for the masa to firm up before serving. Makes 24 tamales.

Muc-bil Pollo
Tamale Pie for Day of the Dead

In all of Latin America, the Day of the Dead (or Dia de los Muertos) is an important celebration that spans roughly from November 1 to 3. Rather than a sad and gloomy occasion, it is a time for festivity, religious rituals, special foods, and fond remembrance of loved ones—a family reunion for both the living and the dearly departed. In Maya lands, this holiday is known as Hanal Pixan, and the customs are reflective of ancient Maya traditions and beliefs in synergy with Catholic practices.

Probably the most recognized of all the dishes prepared for Hanal Pixan in the Yucatán is Muc-bil Pollo. In addition to being served to family and visitors, slices are invariably placed on the altar along with favorite beverages, sweets, flowers, and copal incense, all to entice the deceased family members' spirits to return for a brief sojourn. More of a tamale pie than individually wrapped tamales, Muc-bil Pollo is baked after wrapping it in banana leaves and placing it in an earthenware pot. Tradition calls for cooking in the pib dug in the ground, although these days it is often carried to the local bakery or baked in the home oven. This dish lends itself well to preparing the filling in advance, and once it is in the oven, very little attention is required—perfect for a time of celebration!

Filling

1 pound pork butt or stew meat, cut into 2-inch pieces

10 to 12 cloves garlic, toasted and peeled

1 white onion, cut in half and toasted with the peel on

1 to 2 habañero chiles, charred and left whole

2 sprigs fresh epazote or 1 tablespoon dry

1 tablespoon Mexican oregano, toasted

2 tablespoons sour orange juice or mild fruity vinegar

3 tablespoons achiote paste or Recado Colorado (see page 95)

2 teaspoons salt

½ teaspoon black pepper

2 pounds chicken pieces, bone in

1. For the filling, place the pork in 2 quarts water and add the garlic, onion, chile, herbs, juice, achiote, salt, and pepper. Bring to a boil and cook for 30 minutes. Add the chicken and cook at a slow boil, occasionally skimming any foam off the top, until the chicken is done, about 1 hour.

2. Remove the meat from the broth, cool, and coarsely shred. Strain the broth, reserving 2½ cups for the Kol (gravy) and 1¼ cups for the masa. Save 1 chile for the masa.

3. Make the Kol (gravy) by mixing the reserved masa with 2½ cups broth until smooth. Slowly simmer for about 15 to 20 minutes, or until the Kol has thickened like gravy, and then remove from the heat.

4. Melt the lard, and with a stand mixer or by hand, beat it into the masa alternately with the 1¼ cups broth and the chopped chile and salt until smooth. Fold in the beans if using.

5. Toast the banana leaves to make them pliable (see Techniques, page 16) and tear several into strips as ties.

Masa

Masa for Tamales (see page 34), reserve ¾ cup

¾ pounds pork lard

1 habañero chile from cooking the meats, stemmed, seeded, and finely chopped

1½ teaspoons salt

1½ cups cooked black-eyed peas (optional)

Banana leaves for wrapping, 4 to 5 good-sized pieces or more depending on the size of your pan

2 large tomatoes, sliced

1 sweet bell pepper, seeded and sliced

1 white or red onion, peeled and sliced

Place one leaf in the bottom of a large casserole, Dutch oven, or heavy roasting pan, and then lay the ties in a cross. On top of the ties, line with enough leaves to come up the side and overlap on top.

6. Place two-thirds of the masa in the bottom and up the sides about ½ inch thick. Mix half of the Kol with the meats and place on the masa. Pour remaining Kol over top, and then lay the tomato, pepper, and onion slices over that.

7. Top with the remaining masa and pinch together the edges with the bottom to make a sealed package around the filling. Place a banana leaf on top and fold the edges of the other leaves over that. Tie the pieces of the cross to secure the package.

8. Bake at 375 degrees for 1½ hours. Remove from the oven and allow to sit for 20 to 30 minutes.

9. Cut open the package and carefully open (there will still be some hot steam). Serve family style on the banana leaves or cut into individual portions and garnish with chopped hard-boiled eggs. Makes 10 to 12 servings.

Brazo de la Reina

Queen's Arm Tamale

This is the unusual tamale that I first tasted at Eladio's, a Yucateco restaurant in Mérida, popular with the locals, where white-clad waiters serve authentic antojitos and main dishes under a thatched palapa canopy while live music entertains the diners. The name means "Queen's arm;" the tamale is cooked in one large roll to resemble an arm, and is then usually cut in finger-sized pieces and served on a banana leaf.

2 pounds chaya leaves or spinach, Swiss chard, beet greens, or collard greens, stems removed and cut into pieces 2 inches across

1 teaspoon salt

Masa from Tamalitos Chayas (see page 86), prepared through step 2 and adding the cooked greens to the masa instead of reserving Masa for Tamales (see page 34)

1 cup pork lard, shortening, or a combination of shortening and butter

3 or 4 large banana leaves, plus extra for serving

10 ounces pumpkin seeds, toasted and ground

8 hard-boiled eggs, peeled and cut into ½-inch slices

Charred Chile and Tomato Sauce (see page 119)

1. Cook the chaya leaves in 2 quarts boiling with the salt until they are tender, taking care that they do not become too soft. Drain and reserve 1½ quarts of the cooking water.

2. Mix the masa with the cooled water in which the chaya leaves were cooked. Gently heat this in a heavy saucepan or Dutch oven until it comes to a boil and then add the lard.

3. Cook the mixture, stirring often (a wooden spoon works well for this), for 15 to 20 minutes, or until cooked through and smooth. You can tell it is ready when a small amount is pressed on a banana leaf and it pulls away easily and cleanly. Fold in the chaya leaves.

4. Toast the banana leaves to make them pliable. Lay them out, shiny side up and overlapping, to form a 24 x 12-inch rectangle.

5. Spread the masa evenly in the center of the leaves to form an 8 x 16-inch rectangle.

6. Sprinkle two-thirds of the pumpkin seeds in a 2-inch-wide strip down the center of the masa. Lay the egg slices on top of the pumpkin seeds in one row.

7. Roll up the tamale by first folding the leaf away from you until the two edges of the masa meet. Fold in the two ends to the edge of the masa. Tuck the roll in firmly and finish rolling in a log shape. If necessary, add more banana leaves to ensure the tamale is well sealed. You may use strips of the leaves to secure the tamale.

8. Create a double boiler or bain-marie out of two roasting or other pans that will nest together and accommodate the tamale. Place 1½ inches of water in the first pan, nest the second pan on top, place the tamale in the second pan, and cover with foil or a tight-fitting lid. Bake in the oven at 350 degrees for 50 to 60 minutes. (You may also cook on the stovetop, but be sure you keep water in the pan at all times).

9. Cool the tamale for 10 minutes or so and carefully unwrap.

10. Cut into slices or finger shapes for serving.

11. Place several slices on a banana leaf, top each serving with the warm Charred Chile and Tomato Sauce, and sprinkle with the remaining pumpkin seeds to serve. Makes 8 servings.

SWEET TAMALES

Seldom do most North Americans think of sweet when it comes to tamales.

We usually imagine savory and spicy; however, there are many cooks that prepare the sweet versions. In Mexico, often the term "sweet" or "dulce" is applied to tamales that are not necessarily for dessert but are rather not so spicy, like green corn tamales, or they contain some sweet aromatics like cinnamon, cloves, anise, etc. The recipes that follow are a mix of traditional sweet tamales and contemporary original creations. They work as desserts, breakfast, or brunch accompaniments, or as an interesting side dish in Mexican and Southwestern meals. Sweet tamales are fun to experiment with, and after you have given a few of these a try, you may find yourself inventing tamale versions of your favorite sweet things.

Tamales de Anís

Anise and Dried Fruit Tamales

My first taste of these tamales happened the day I met Doña Angela in Xalapa, Veracruz. We had them for breakfast along with some savory tamales and a peanut-chipotle salsa. It might seem unusual to combine the sweet tamales with the rather hot salsa, but it really goes together well. I have created my own version, using tips I have acquired from several Veracruzana tamaleras.

They are simple yet rich and sweet. There is no filling required; everything is mixed in the masa. You could leave out the fruit, add or substitute cloves and canela (cinnamon) for the aniseeds, and also add nuts if you like. Some cooks use milk or natas, the foamy substance that forms between fresh cream and milk, in place of water to give them a softer texture and extra richness. These tamales work great as a breakfast or brunch item or as a dessert when served with a vanilla sauce or whipped cream.

Sweet Masa (see page 41)

2 tablespoons aniseeds, lightly toasted

¾ cup raisins, chopped prunes, or other dried fruit

24 corn husks, soaked, plus extra for ties and covering in the steamer

Salsa de Cacahuate con Chipotle
(Peanut and Chipotle Chile Salsa)

1 cup raw peanuts

1 tablespoon vegetable or peanut oil

½ medium onion, dry roasted

3 cloves garlic, peeled and roasted

1 to 2 chipotle chiles en adobo

3 medium tomatoes, well roasted

1 tablespoon apple cider vinegar

2 tablespoons cold water or more as needed

⅛ cup chopped cilantro

Salt to taste

1. Add the aniseeds along with the liquid in step 3 of the masa recipe. Fold in the raisins after completing the float test in step 4 of the masa recipe.

2. Place about 2 well-rounded tablespoons of masa on the center of each corn husk.

3. Fold one side of the husk over, roll up, and then tie each tail with a strip of husk (see Assembly, page 20).

4. Arrange on their sides in a preheated steamer pot, leaving room for the steam to circulate (use the extra husks to cover the tamales in the steamer).

5. Steam for 45 minutes to 1 hour, or until the masa has firmed somewhat and pulls away from the husk easily.

6. Turn off the heat, remove the covering husks, and let rest for 15 to 20 minutes before serving.

7. For the salsa, fry the peanuts in the oil until golden brown, about 3 minutes.

8. Grind all ingredients except the cilantro and salt in a molcajete or blender until somewhat smooth yet still grainy.

9. Stir in the cilantro and salt. Makes 24 to 30 tamales.

Tamales de Piña y Coco
Pineapple and Coconut Tamales

These tamales are decidedly tropical and sweet enough to be dessert, but I like to serve them as a side to accompany spicy pork or chicken dishes. Either way, they are a crowd-pleaser and fairly quick to put together. Try adding a finely chopped chile habañero or a couple of teaspoons of bottled habañero sauce to the masa for a mind-blowing variation. The heat of the chile is toned down by the sweetness of the fruit, and the flavors are very complementary.

Sweet Masa (see page 41) using only ¼ cup sugar and 1 (13-ounce) can coconut milk instead of the water

¾ cup sweetened and shredded coconut

2½ cups diced fresh pineapple or pineapple chunks in water, drained

3 tablespoons medium brown sugar or grated Mexican piloncillo

½ teaspoon ground allspice (optional)

1 generous dash ground cloves (optional)

24 corn husks, soaked, plus extra for ties and covering in the steamer

1. Fold in the shredded coconut after completing the float test in step 4 of the masa recipe.

2. Mix the pineapple chunks with the brown sugar and the spices (if using).

3. Spread the masa about ⅜ inch thick on the smooth side of the corn husks to cover the widest two-thirds of the husk to within ½ inch of each side (see Assembly, page 18).

4. Place about 2 tablespoons filling in the center of the masa on each husk.

5. Fold one side of the husk over to meet the masa on the other side, roll up, and then fold the tails (see Assembly, page 20).

6. Arrange upright if possible (to prevent losing any juices) in a preheated steamer pot, leaving room for the steam to circulate (use the extra husks to cover the tamales in the steamer).

7. Steam for 1 to 1¼ hours, or until the masa has firmed somewhat and pulls away from the husk easily.

8. Turn off the heat, remove the covering husks, and let rest for 15 to 20 minutes before serving. Makes 24 to 30 tamales.

Tamales de Chocolate Mexicano y Almendras

Mexican Chocolate and Almond Tamales

Mirroring the flavors of the classic Mexican hot chocolate drink, cacao, canela, and toasted almonds, these tamales are scandalously delicious. Serve them with coffee or tea in the morning, as part of an elaborate breakfast or brunch, as dessert, or just as a self-indulgent treat. If you prefer to ration them, they freeze well and then they may be reheated directly from the freezer by steaming or microwaving. Serve as they are or top with whipped cream and/or warm chocolate sauce.

Sweet Masa (see page 41), using only ¼ cup sugar and 12 ounces Mexican chocolate (my favorite is Mayordomo, made in Oaxaca), or semisweet chocolate chips melted in 1 cup strong coffee or water as the liquid

1 teaspoon ground canela (sweet Sri Lanka cinnamon)

1 teaspoon Mexican vanilla extract or other premium vanilla (optional)

¾ cup sliced or slivered almonds, toasted golden brown

24 corn husks, soaked, plus extra for ties and covering in the steamer

1. Add the canela and vanilla along with the liquid in step 3 of the masa recipe.

2. Fold in the almonds after completing the float test in step 4 of the masa recipe.

3. Place about 2 well-rounded tablespoons masa on the center of each corn husk.

4. Fold one side of the husk over, roll up, and then tie each tail with a strip of husk (see Assembly, page 20).

5. Arrange on their sides in a preheated steamer pot, leaving room for the steam to circulate (use the extra husks to cover the tamales in the steamer).

6. Steam for 45 minutes to 1 hour, or until the masa has firmed somewhat and pulls away from the husk easily.

7. Turn off the heat, remove the covering husks, and let rest for 15 to 20 minutes before serving. Makes 24 to 30 tamales.

Tamale Dulce con Chocolate, Nuez y Cereza

Chunky Dark Chocolate, Cherry, and Pecan Tamale

Another decadent modern take on tamales, these may be served warm out of the steamer but also taste great when cool. Almost a candy, they make a remarkable dessert. You may substitute different fruits or eliminate them altogether, choose a different type of nut, or exchange some of the dark chocolate for white chocolate to make variations. For a double chocolate fantasy, add 3 tablespoons cocoa powder to the masa when you prepare it.

Sweet Masa (see page 41), prepared using 100 percent butter

12 ounces bittersweet or semisweet chocolate, cut into chunks (or use chips)

1¼ cups pecans, lightly toasted and coarsely chopped

1½ cups dried sour cherries

2 teaspoons Mexican vanilla extract or other premium vanilla

24 corn husks, soaked, plus extra for ties and covering in the steamer

1. Fold in the chocolate, pecans, cherries, and vanilla after completing the float test in step 4 of the masa recipe.

2. Place about 2 heaping tablespoons masa on the center of each corn husk.

3. Fold one side of the husk over, roll up, and then tie each tail with a strip of husk (see Assembly, page 20).

4. Arrange the tamales on their sides in a preheated steamer pot, leaving room for the steam to circulate (use the extra husks to cover the tamales in the steamer).

5. Steam for 45 minutes to 1 hour, or until the masa has firmed somewhat and pulls away from the husk easily.

6. Turn off the heat, remove the covering husks, and let rest for 15 to 20 minutes before serving. Makes 24 to 30 tamales.

SAUCES & SALSAS

Along with the meats, seafood, and vegetables that are used to fill tamales, a separate sauce or salsa is often added for flavor, color, and extra moisture.

In this chapter, I have included traditional sauces and my own contemporary creations. They are called for in the recipes in the Tamales chapter of this book, and they may also serve as inspiration to your own original creations. Traditionally in Mexico and Central America, the sauce is placed in the tamale, and rarely is there a sauce added after the tamales are cooked. If, like many North Americans, you like to serve extra sauce after the tamales are unwrapped, just make some extra for that purpose.

Mole Negro Oaxaqueño
Black Mole Oaxaca-Style

This sauce is the grandmother of all moles, and I would be remiss if I omitted it here. Granted, it is complicated and time-consuming to prepare; however, if you aspire to the pinnacle of tamale preparation, you will want to make it sometime. In Oaxaca, this mole is saved for special occasions, above all for the Dia de los Muertos or Day of the Dead, and can be served with chicken or turkey or used for tamales with either type of poultry (many cooks will make more than enough to serve for one special meal and then use the leftovers to make the tamales or to keep on hand to offer to drop-in guests during this festive time). You could prepare a smaller quantity; however, it is almost as easy to make more. And, since it freezes well, why not make the whole recipe? You will find that it is used fairly quickly.

1 teaspoon allspice

½ teaspoon cloves

½ teaspoon black peppercorns

1 (2-inch) piece canela (cinnamon)

6 chiles mulatos (ancho negro black), stemmed and seeded (reserve the seeds)

4 to 5 chiles chilhuacles negros (if you can't get chilhuacles, just increase the other varieties accordingly), stemmed and seeded

6 chiles guajillos, stemmed and seeded

4 to 5 chiles pasillas negros, stemmed and seeded

1 to 2 dry chipotle chiles (the brown Meco is the best here), stemmed and seeded

1 slice egg bread (pan de yema or challah) or baguette

6 tablespoons pork lard or vegetable oil, divided

2 stale corn tortillas, cut in small pieces

¼ cup whole almonds

1. Toast the allspice, cloves, peppercorns, and canela in a dry pan until the aroma of the spices is noticeable; grind, and set aside.

2. Toast the chile seeds until very dark (do not be too concerned about burning these seeds, they need to be almost black to provide color and a touch of bitterness); grind, and add to the ground spices.

3. Toast the chiles (both sides) in the pan until fairly dark in color, place in a bowl, and cover with boiling water. Soak for 20 minutes and remove from the water.

4. In a preheated heavy skillet or Dutch oven, fry the bread in 2 tablespoons of the lard until dark brown on both sides. Do the same with the tortillas until almost blackened.

5. Add 2 more tablespoons lard and fry the nuts and plantain together until the plantain is golden brown; add the raisins and sesame seeds, and continue frying, stirring constantly, until the raisins have become well plumped. Remove from the pan.

6. Combine all of the ingredients except the broth, remaining lard, salt, and chocolate.

7. Divide in two or three parts and blend each part with 1 quart broth until very smooth. (Add more broth as needed

¼ cup whole raw peanuts, skinned

¼ cup pecan halves

1 ripe plantain, peeled and sliced

⅛ cup raisins

2 tablespoons sesame seeds

1 pound tomatoes, pan roasted until well blackened

5 ounces tomatillos (4 to 5 medium-sized), husked, rinsed, and pan roasted until well blackened

1 large white onion, peeled, cut in thirds, and pan roasted until slightly charred

10 cloves garlic, pan roasted until slightly blackened, and then peeled

2 teaspoons dry oregano (Oaxaca or Mexican), toasted

2½ quarts rich chicken broth

1½ teaspoons salt

5 ounces Mexican chocolate

to free the blender but take care not to add more than is needed to blend).

8. Heat the remaining 2 tablespoons lard in a heavy pot or pan (large enough to easily accommodate the entire mole.

9. Strain the puree into the hot lard and fry, stirring occasionally for 5 to 7 minutes, or until the mixture has begun to thicken and darken a bit. Reduce heat to simmer (adding additional broth to thin from time to time) and cook, stirring occasionally, for 20 to 30 minutes, or until the mole is the consistency of thin gravy and the flavors are well combined. Add half of the salt, taste, and add more as desired.

10. Break the chocolate into chunks, add to the sauce, and cook for 5 minutes more while stirring.

11. Serve with poached or roasted chicken or turkey garnished with additional toasted sesame seeds, along with plain white rice, or use in the recipe for Black Mole Tamales (see page 90). Makes enough for 30 to 40 tamales.

Salsa Verde
Green Sauce

This is basic Mexican table and taquería salsa is simple and straightforward, and may be used with tamales, enchiladas, chilaquiles, tacos, or simply as a table salsa or dip. The amount of chile heat is controlled by the varieties and quantities of chiles used. This sauce tends to thicken with time; add water to restore its original consistency.

1 teaspoon salt

1 pound tomatillos, husked and rinsed

2 to 3 fresh jalapeño or serrano chiles, stemmed and cut in half, or 2 hot green New Mexican chiles or 1 habañero chile, stemmed and seeded

1 medium white onion, peeled and roughly chopped

3 cloves garlic, toasted and peeled

⅛ cup chopped cilantro leaves

1. Place enough water in a pot or saucepan to cover the tomatillos and bring to a boil.

2. Add the salt and tomatillos and cook for 10 minutes; drain.

3. Place everything in a blender and coarsely puree. Makes about 2½ cups.

NOTE: If the salsa is a little too tart, mix in about ½ teaspoon sugar.

Salsa Rojo Norteño
Northern-Style Red Sauce

If you grew up in the United States, especially in California, Texas, or Arizona, your first encounter with tamales probably included this sauce. There are regional variations, but it is usually based on mild ancho chiles with some tomato and has its roots in the northern parts of Mexico. In some areas, the sauce is more brown than red as ancho chiles can vary widely in color. Make sure they are ancho rojo and not mulatto or negro variations if you want a good red color. Like many of the sauces here, this one also doubles as an enchilada sauce.

2 medium white onions, roughly chopped

8 to 10 cloves garlic, peeled

3 tablespoons vegetable oil or lard

8 to 10 ancho chiles, stemmed, seeded, toasted, and then soaked in boiling water for 15 minutes and drained*

2 cups pan-roasted and pureed tomatoes or canned tomato puree

1 quart chicken, pork, or vegetable broth

1½ teaspoons toasted and ground cumin seed

2 teaspoons salt

1 to 2 tablespoons sugar or honey

1 teaspoon, Mexican oregano, toasted (optional)

1. In a tall pot or Dutch oven, sauté the onions and garlic with the oil until beginning to brown. Remove from heat and take the onion and garlic out with a slotted spoon, leaving the oil in the pot.

2. Puree the onions, garlic, soaked chiles, and tomato with a little of the broth.

3. Reheat the oil and fry the chile mixture for 3 to 4 minutes to develop the flavor, stirring regularly.

4. Add the cumin, salt, sugar, oregano (if using), and enough broth to make a thin gravy.

5. Simmer for 15 to 20 minutes, adding more broth as needed. Taste and adjust for salt and sugar. Makes about 7 cups.

*If you want a hotter sauce substitute, add a few New Mexico or California red chiles, or just add a few extra chile pequin or chile de arbol.

Salsa de Ajo
Garlic Salsa

This is a slightly milder version of the incendiary Chile Tamulado, due to the inclusion of lots of roasted garlic and fewer chiles; but be careful, it is still fairly hot and may be considered tongue-numbing by chile novices. Mixed with pork, turkey, chicken, or seafood for tamales, it may also be used as an accompaniment for tamales or as a table sauce for the brave.

2 to 3 habañero chiles (green if you can find them) or other hot green chiles, well-charred and stemmed

12 to 16 cloves garlic, pan roasted and skinned

2 (¼-inch-thick) round slices of white onion, pan roasted and diced fine (optional)

½ teaspoon toasted Mexican oregano (optional)

2 to 3 tablespoons sour orange juice, or a mix of lime juice and mild vinegar

Dash of salt

1. Smash all of the ingredients together in a molcajete or mortar and pestle, adding the juice as needed to make a semi-smooth paste. Makes about 1 cup (if using onions).

New Mexico Red Chile Sauce

This is the classic chile sauce from New Mexico, where I live, and is one answer to the state question: "red or green?" In addition to figuring in several tamale recipes that I use, it is great for enchiladas, huevos rancheros, and chile rellenos, or in a bowl with beans and flour tortillas on the side. It also is used for the legendary Frito Pie, first created in the Woolworth's on the plaza in Santa Fe. Many versions contain only the chiles and some garlic, perhaps some onion, but I like to add a bit more spices and some technique from south of the border. It is still very simple to create. For a pure chile flavor, use the water-only option; for a richer sauce, use the broth. For a smooth chile sauce, blend everything in a blender after cooking.

1 medium white onion, peeled and diced

2 tablespoons vegetable oil or pork lard

5 cloves garlic, finely chopped (add more if you like)

1 tablespoon masa harina or 1½ teaspoons all-purpose flour

¾ to 1 cup New Mexican red chile powder (hot or mild), lightly toasted*

1 teaspoon cumin seeds, toasted and ground

1 tablespoon Mexican oregano, toasted

1 teaspoon salt

4 cups water, chicken broth or pork broth

1 or 2 teaspoons honey (optional, helps to balance the chile heat)

1. Saute onion in oil until a little color develops; add the garlic and continue cooking for 1 minute. Add the masa harina and cook, stirring constantly for 1 minute more.

2. Add the chile, spices, salt, and water, whisking well to blend smooth.

3. Reduce heat and simmer for 15 to 20 minutes more, stirring occasionally (add more liquid as needed if the sauce gets too thick). Makes 6 cups.

NOTE: To make this recipe using whole chile pods, merely stem, seed, and toast the chiles; then cover in boiling water and soak for 15 minutes. Puree the chiles in the blender with just enough plain water to free the blades. Add the puree when the powder is called for in the recipe.

*Make sure to use pure chile powder that does not contain any other spices.

Chiltomate

Charred Chile and Tomato Sauce

This salsa forms the basis of many recipes throughout the Maya regions of Mexico. It is a simple blend of tomatoes and chiles. There are many variations; the most traditional cook uses only the molcajete to puree everything, but in modern times the blender has been utilized. Most cooks roast the ingredients, but some boil everything. Some versions are strained, but most are left a little chunky. Some cooks use onions and garlic while others use only tomatoes and chiles; and, finally, some fry the salsa after it is assembled to intensify and sweeten the flavor, and others use it as is. Feel free to exercise your own judgment or just follow the directions in the recipe that calls for the chiltomate. The most common chile for this salsa is the habañero; however, in Chiapas, Tabasco, Guatemala, and Belize, you will often see a different fresh green chile utilized and the results can be a little milder—again, your choice. Although, included here for tamales, the rich, complex flavors and the brightness of the chiles along with the exotic aroma of the epazote or the brightness of cilantro are a great accompaniment to grilled or smoked meats and seafood, served on tacos or chiles rellenos, or just used as a table salsa for dipping chips when made with cilantro.

About 1 pound ripe tomatoes

1 habañero, serrano, New Mexican green, or jalapeño chile

1 small white onion, peeled and thickly sliced (optional)

2 cloves garlic (optional)

3 to 4 epazote leaves or ⅛ cup chopped cilantro leaves

⅓ cup sour orange juice, or ¼ cup sweet orange juice mixed with 2 tablespoons mild vinegar

½ teaspoon salt

1. Grill the tomatoes, chile, onion, and garlic (if using) on a comal or heavy skillet until slightly blackened.

2. Stem and seed the chile, chop the onion, and peel the garlic.

3. Coarsely mash the tomatoes, chile, onion, and garlic in a molcajete or with a mortar and pestle, or pulse in a food processor or blender.

4. Mix in the epazote, orange juice, and salt. Makes about 2½ cups.

Salsa Veracruzana
Smoky Chipotle Tomato Sauce Veracruz Style

I learned how to make this sauce in Veracruz, Mexico. It is fairly quick to make and the smoky earthiness of the chipotles will complement many types of Mexican dishes. When the Veracruzanos make it, they often simmer a few leaves of acuyo (hoja santa) in the sauce to add the anise-like flavor of that well-loved herb to the salsa. I have had good luck in imitating this subtle flavor using aniseed, since the acuyo can be difficult to find north of the border. Fresh roasted and peeled jalapeño chiles may also be substituted for the chipotle chiles for a different variation. These options are all delicious.

2 to 3 dry chipotle chiles (meco or mora) or chipotle chiles en adobo

2 pounds ripe tomatoes

5 cloves garlic, peeled

1 large or 2 medium white onions, peeled and cut into ⅜-inch-thick rounds

2 teaspoons mild vinegar (apple cider or rice works best)

2 to 3 leaves acuyo (hoja santa), or ½ teaspoon aniseed, lightly toasted and ground (optional)

2 tablespoons vegetable oil

1½ teaspoons salt

Water as needed

Juice of 1 lime

Handful of chopped cilantro (optional)

1. If using the dry chipotle chiles, toast them in a dry pan; then stem, seed, and cover with boiling water to soak for 15 minutes.

2. Pan-roast the tomatoes, garlic, and onion slices until the tomatoes are fairly well charred and the onions are blackening around the edges. Dice the onions and set aside.

3. Place the garlic in a blender to puree along with the tomatoes, vinegar, and chiles.

4. Heat the oil in a pan and fry the puree for 2 to 3 minutes. Add the onions, acuyo, and salt. Reduce the heat and simmer 10 minutes, adding water if needed to keep the sauce from drying out and scorching. Remove from the heat, place in a bowl, and cool for a few minutes. Remove the acuyo leaves if using.

5. Add the lime juice and cilantro and stir well. Taste for salt. May be served warm or at room temperature. Makes about 5 cups.

Salsa para Tamales Tropicales
Tropical Chile Sauce for Tamales

This is a sauce that I developed using recipes that I learned from several different cooks in regions around southern Mexico. It has a lot of the flavors and complexity of a mole without the difficulty level of most mole recipes. The achiote gives the sauce a deeper red color and a subtle flavor boost but is not essential if you do not have any. This sauce works great for many tamale recipes and as an enchilada sauce or with poultry. It also freezes well.

2 tablespoons vegetable oil

1 banana (not too ripe)

8 medium ancho chiles, toasted, seeded, soaked in hot water for 15 minutes, and then drained

1 or 2 chipotle chiles en adobo

1 white onion, peeled and sliced into 3 rounds and pan-roasted

10 cloves garlic, pan-roasted and then peeled

8 medium tomatoes, charred

6 epazote leaves, or 1 tablespoon dried epazote

2 teaspoons Mexican oregano, toasted

2 teaspoons whole allspice, toasted and ground

1 ounce achiote paste (optional)

1 (2-inch) piece canela (cinnamon), ground (about 2 teaspoons)

Pinch of ground cloves

Broth or water as needed (about 4 cups or so)

1 teaspoon salt

1. Heat the oil in a tall-sided heavy pan or Dutch oven on high heat. Slice the banana and fry in the oil until golden brown.

2. Blend the banana, chiles, onion, garlic, tomatoes, herbs, and spices with just enough broth or water to make blending possible.

3. Strain the chile puree into the hot oil and stir constantly for about 2 minutes. Add enough broth or water to achieve the consistency of thin spaghetti sauce, reduce the heat, and simmer for 15 to 20 minutes, stirring occasionally.

4. Add the salt and more liquid if needed, taste, and adjust. Makes about 7 cups.

New Mexico Green Chile Sauce

Life in New Mexico without this sauce seems unimaginable. The green chiles of New Mexico are unique to the area, and no other chile can mimic its flavors. It is a fall ritual in the state to roast and peel enough to put in the freezer for the winter, as they are not available fresh year-round. The aroma can be intoxicating. An acceptable substitute could be poblano chiles or Anaheim chiles with some added jalapeño for heat; however, I usually opt for a different sauce when I do not have these toothsome and piquant specimens. This sauce is usually used for enchiladas, as a base for green chile stew, to smother burritos, and for tamales (both inside and out).

2 cups diced white onions (about 2 medium onions)

2 tablespoons vegetable oil

4 cloves garlic, minced

1 tablespoon masa harina, or 2 teaspoons all-purpose flour

3 cups roasted, peeled, and diced New Mexican green chiles (about 10 to 12 chiles if fresh; otherwise, frozen is fine)

6 cups cool chicken, pork, or vegetable broth, divided

Salt to taste

½ teaspoon freshly ground black pepper

½ teaspoon coriander seeds, toasted and ground (optional)

½ cup diced tomatoes (optional)

⅛ cup chopped cilantro (optional; not traditional but adds a nice touch)

1. Sauté the onions in hot oil until beginning to brown around the edges; add the garlic and cook until the garlic begins to brown.

2. Sprinkle in the masa harina and continue cooking and stirring for about 1 minute more.

3. Add the chiles, 3 cups broth, salt, pepper, and coriander; stir well to combine and bring to a gentle boil. Add 2 cups remaining broth and simmer for 12 to 15 minutes, adding more broth as needed. NOTE: If using tomatoes, add them during the last 5 minutes.

4. Remove from the heat and stir in the cilantro. Makes about 9 cups.

Salsa de Miltomates Asados
Charred Tomatillo Salsa

Tomatillos, or miltomates as they are known in many parts of Mexico, are a tart lemony fruit that grows in a papery husk and is only very distantly related to a tomato. Cooking tends to sweeten the tomatillos and charring them also adds a smokiness that complements the chiles. The choices of chiles are many; the region or the season often dictates the choice. Along with the guajillo or chipotle chiles listed in the recipe, you could also use pasilla, pequin, New Mexico Red, cascabel, chiltepin, pasilla de Oaxaca, or chiles de arbol. Blend the salsa in a molcajete or pulse in a food processor for table sauce or dipping, and blend it smooth with a blender when using in dishes like tamales.

1 pound tomatillos, husked and rinsed

3 to 4 chiles guajillos or chipotle secos, toasted, stemmed, seeded, soaked in boiling water for 15 minutes, drained and then coarsely chopped, or 4 to 5 chipotle chiles en adobo (canned), coarsely chopped

4 to 5 garlic cloves, pan-roasted, peeled, and chopped

2 (¼-inch-thick) slices onion, pan-roasted until slightly charred and then chopped (optional)

½ to 1 teaspoon salt

½ teaspoon sugar, divided

¼ cup water

⅛ cup chopped cilantro (optional)

1. Char-grill, broil, or pan-roast the tomatillos on high heat until fairly blackened.

2. Blend the chiles with the tomatillos, garlic, onion (if using), salt, half the sugar, and the water in a molcajete, food processor, or blender, depending on the texture you desire.

3. Taste for tartness and add more sugar if needed.

4. Stir in the cilantro if using. Makes about 2½ cups.

Caldo de Pollo
Chicken Broth

While not a sauce by itself, chicken broth is important in tamale production and is a component of many tamale sauces. This broth is also used as a base for many soups, stews, sauces, rice dishes, and also tamale masa. The only essential ingredient is the chicken bones; however, the aromatics do add a certain depth of flavor. You may pick and choose from the seasonings as availability dictates or according to your personal tastes. The broth freezes well, and if you put it in ice cube trays and then place the cubes in plastic bags to keep in the freezer, you may easily get the quantities that you need for a particular recipe.

2 to 3 bones from leftover roasted chickens with skin and meat removed, each broken into 4 or 5 pieces

2 medium onions, quartered

3 to 4 carrots, peeled and roughly chopped

3 cloves garlic, peeled

3 ribs celery, cut into 3-inch sections

4 to 5 bay leaves, toasted

1 to 2 sprigs each: fresh marjoram, thyme, epazote, parsley, and cilantro

1 teaspoon allspice berries, toasted

2 teaspoons whole black peppercorns, lightly toasted

2 tablespoons salt

Enough cold water to cover the bones and aromatics (about 6 to 8 quarts)

1. Place all of the ingredients in a stockpot or large kettle and slowly bring to a boil. Occasionally skim the surface to remove any foam or small particles that are produced.

2. Boil for 15 minutes and remove from heat for 15 to 20 minutes. Add 1 quart very cold water and let sit for 5 minutes more.

3. Without stirring, skim again to remove any surface scum, particles, or fat that is on the top.

4. Reheat to a slow boil and cook for 1½ to 2 hours. If the level of the liquid drops below the top of the bones, add more cold water as needed and proceed with cooking.

5. Remove from heat and cool for 20 to 30 minutes.

6. Remove the bones and strain broth through a sieve or colander lined with cheesecloth.

7. Chill the strained broth completely and skim the fat from the surface. Makes about 5 to 6 quarts.

NOTE: After defatting, you may reheat the broth and reduce by one-third to concentrate the flavors more or reduce even more to conserve space when storing.

Kol
Maya Gravy

Kol is a type of gravy that is made from masa, seasonings, and meat broth, and is added to the filling in tamales to add moisture and flavor. It is used throughout the Maya lands of Mexico and Central America.

2 teaspoons achiote paste or Recado
  Colorado (see page 95)
1 cup meat broth or chicken broth
½ cup diced onion
2 teaspoons lard or vegetable oil
½ cup chopped tomato
1 tablespoon chopped epazote
¼ cup Masa for Tamales (see page 34)

1. Dissolve the achiote paste in the broth.

2. Saute onion in the lard until slightly browned, add tomato, epazote, and broth.

3. Bring to a boil and mix in the masa until smooth. If you are using shredded meat for a tamale recipe, add it now and remove from the heat. Follow the recipe directions for the tamale. Makes about 2 cups.

Index

Metric Conversion Chart

Liquid and Dry Measures

U.S.	Canadian	Australian
¼ teaspoon	1 mL	1 ml
½ teaspoon	2 mL	2 ml
1 teaspoon	5 mL	5 ml
1 tablespoon	15 mL	20 ml
¼ cup	50 mL	60 ml
⅓ cup	75 mL	80 ml
½ cup	125 mL	125 ml
⅔ cup	150 mL	170 ml
¾ cup	175 mL	190 ml
1 cup	250 mL	250 ml
1 quart	1 liter	1 litre

Temperature Conversion Chart

Fahrenheit	Celsius
250	120
275	140
300	150
325	160
350	180
375	190
400	200
425	220
450	230
475	240
500	260